BEGINNER

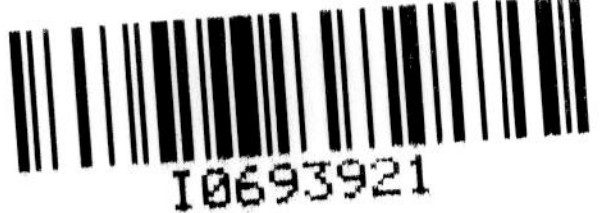

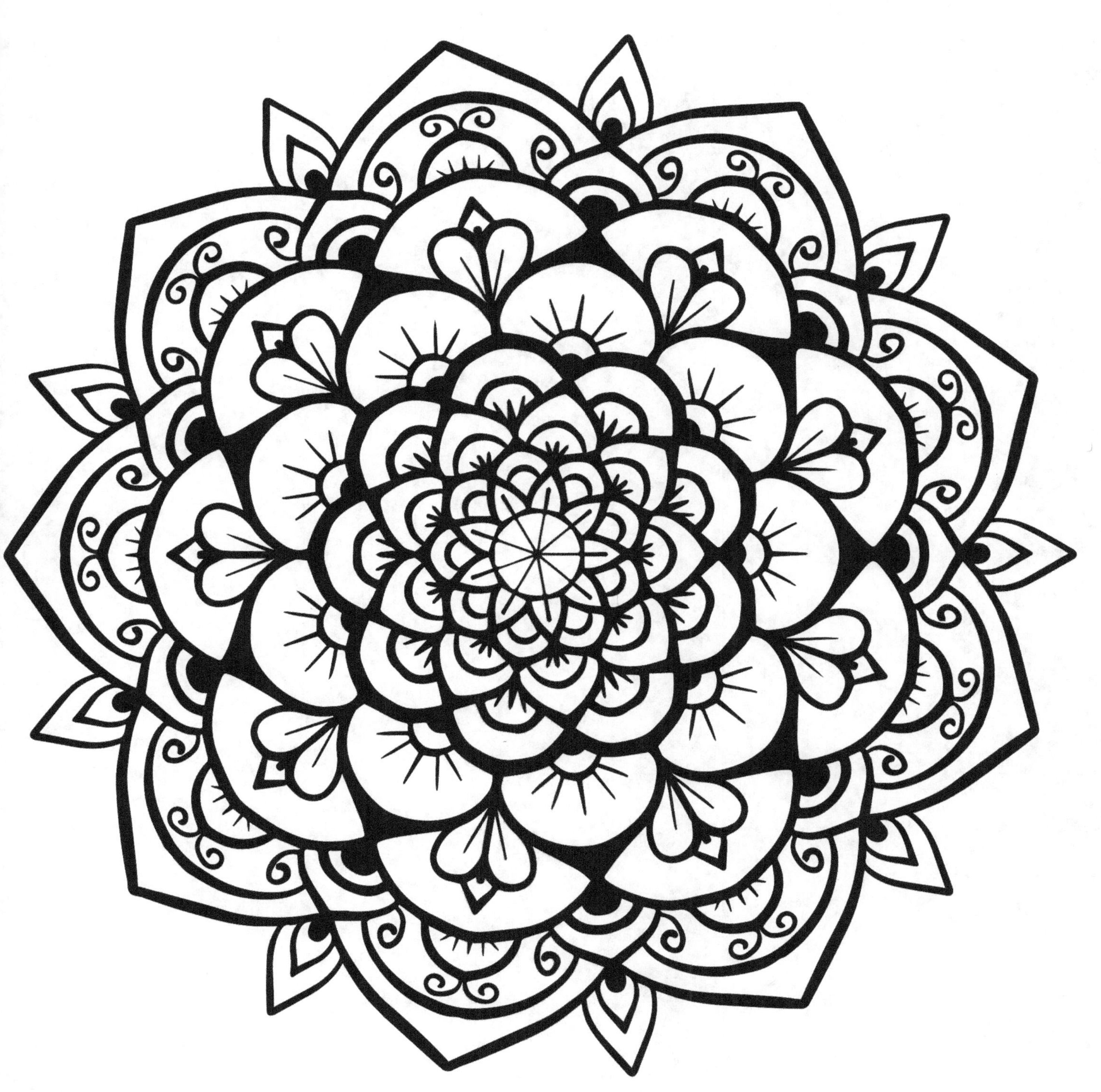

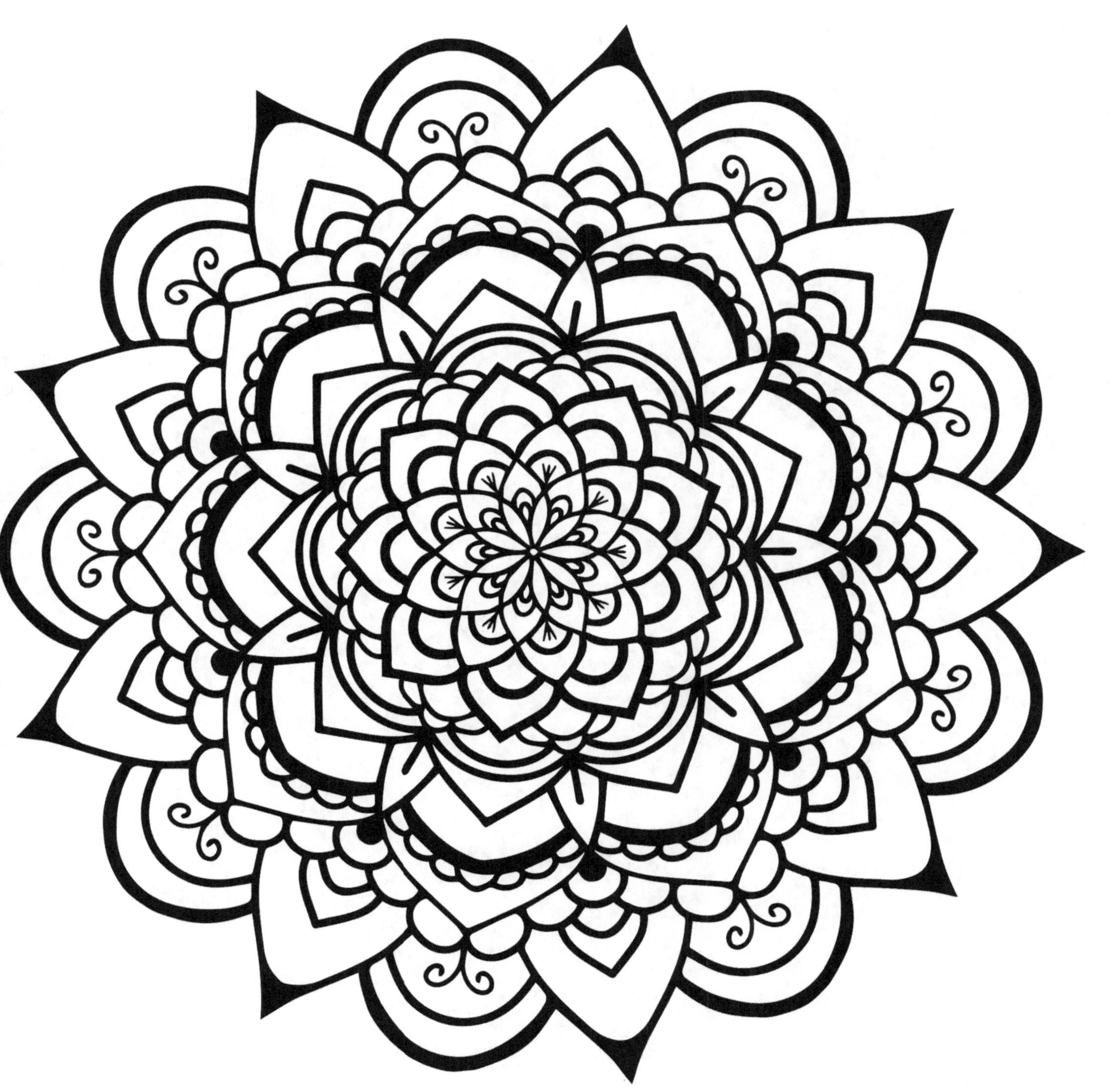

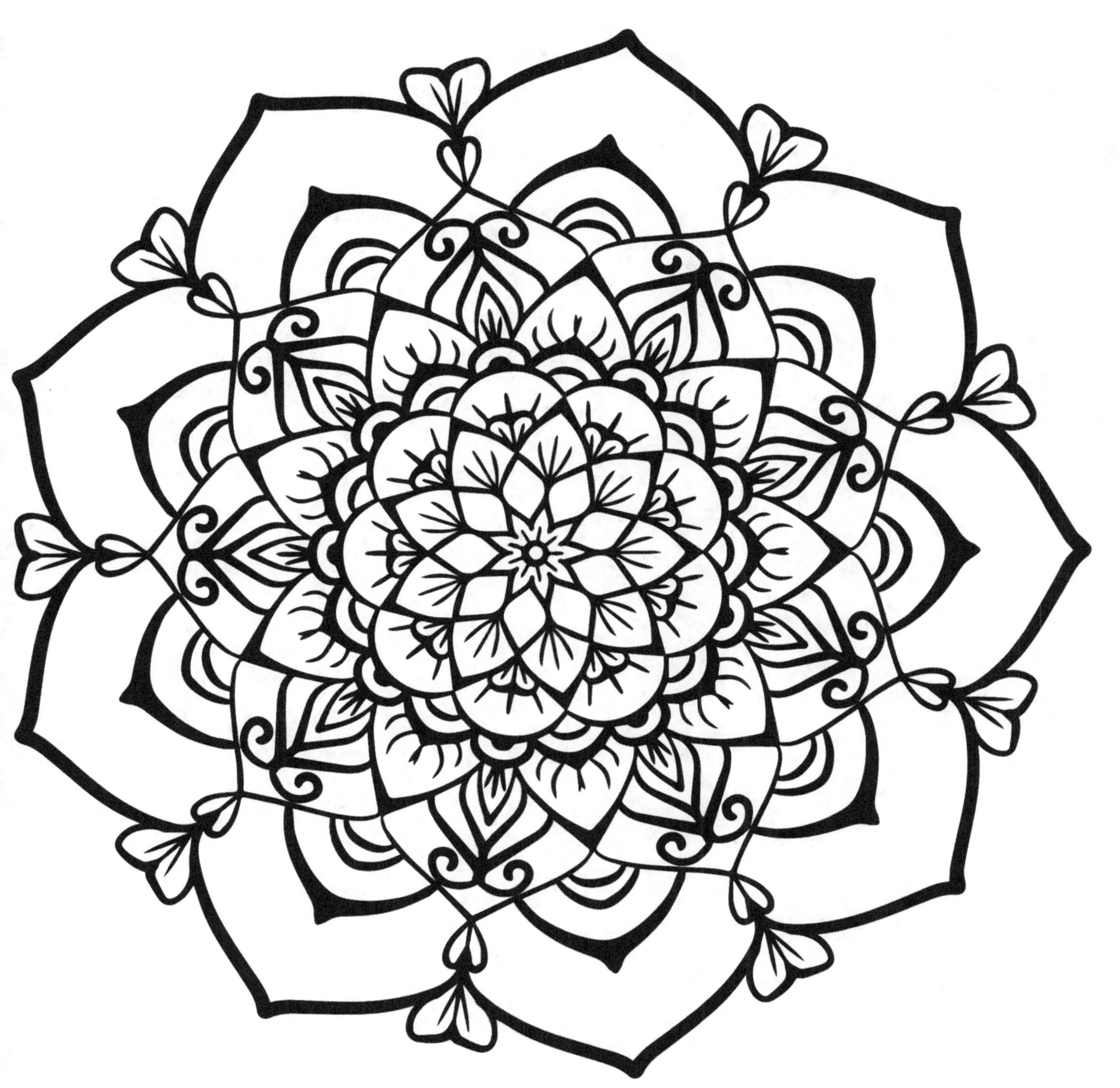

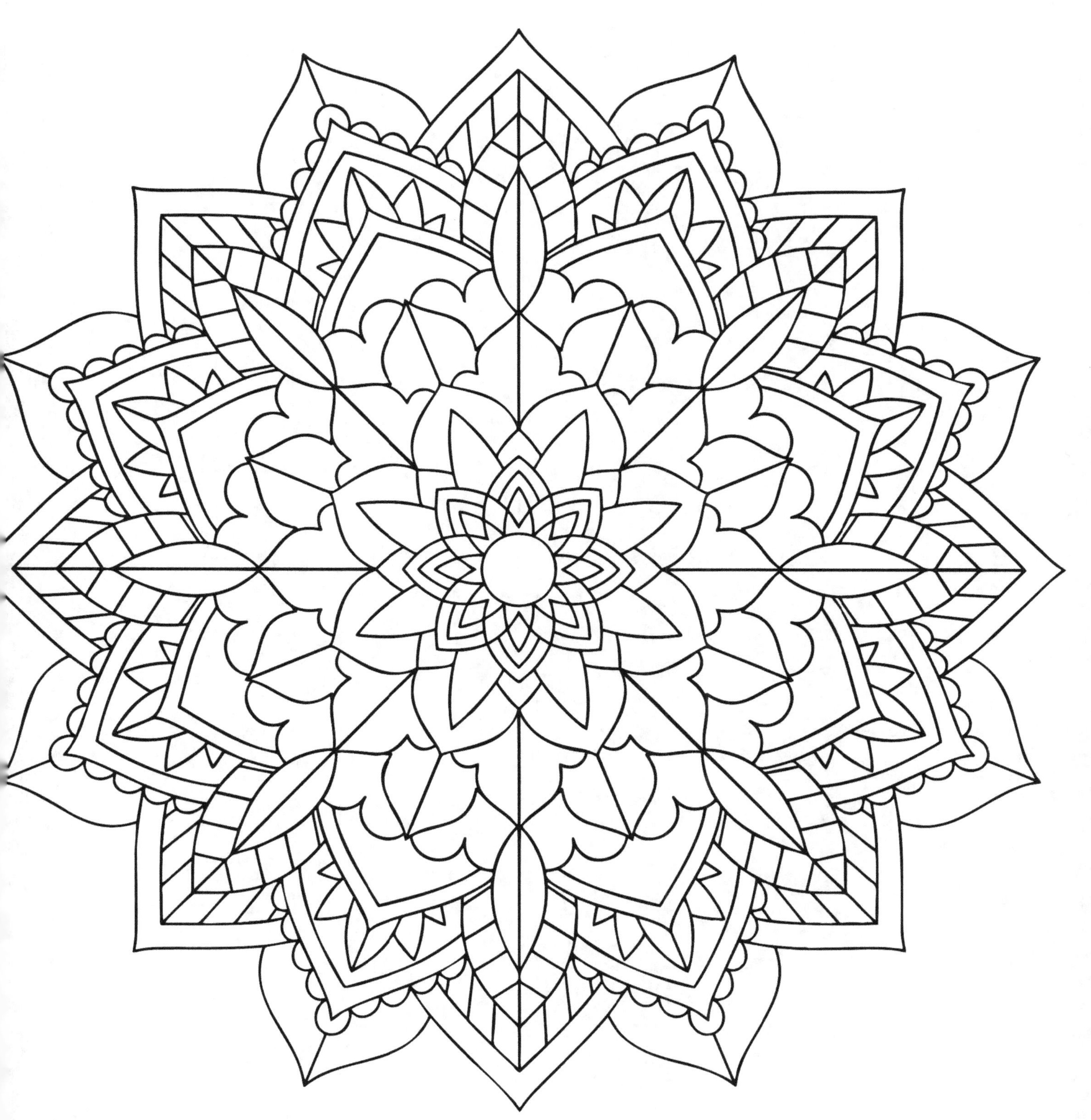

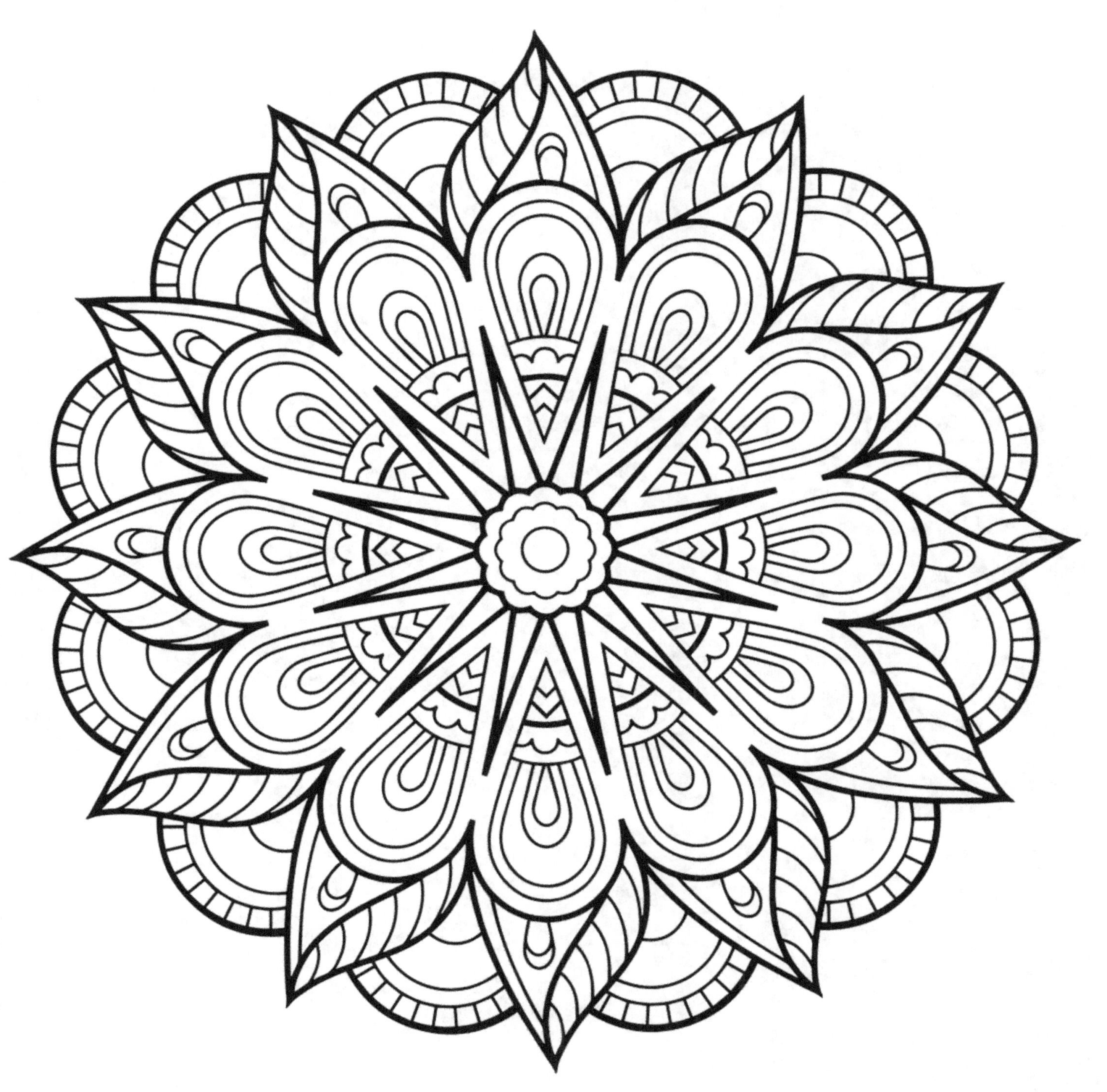

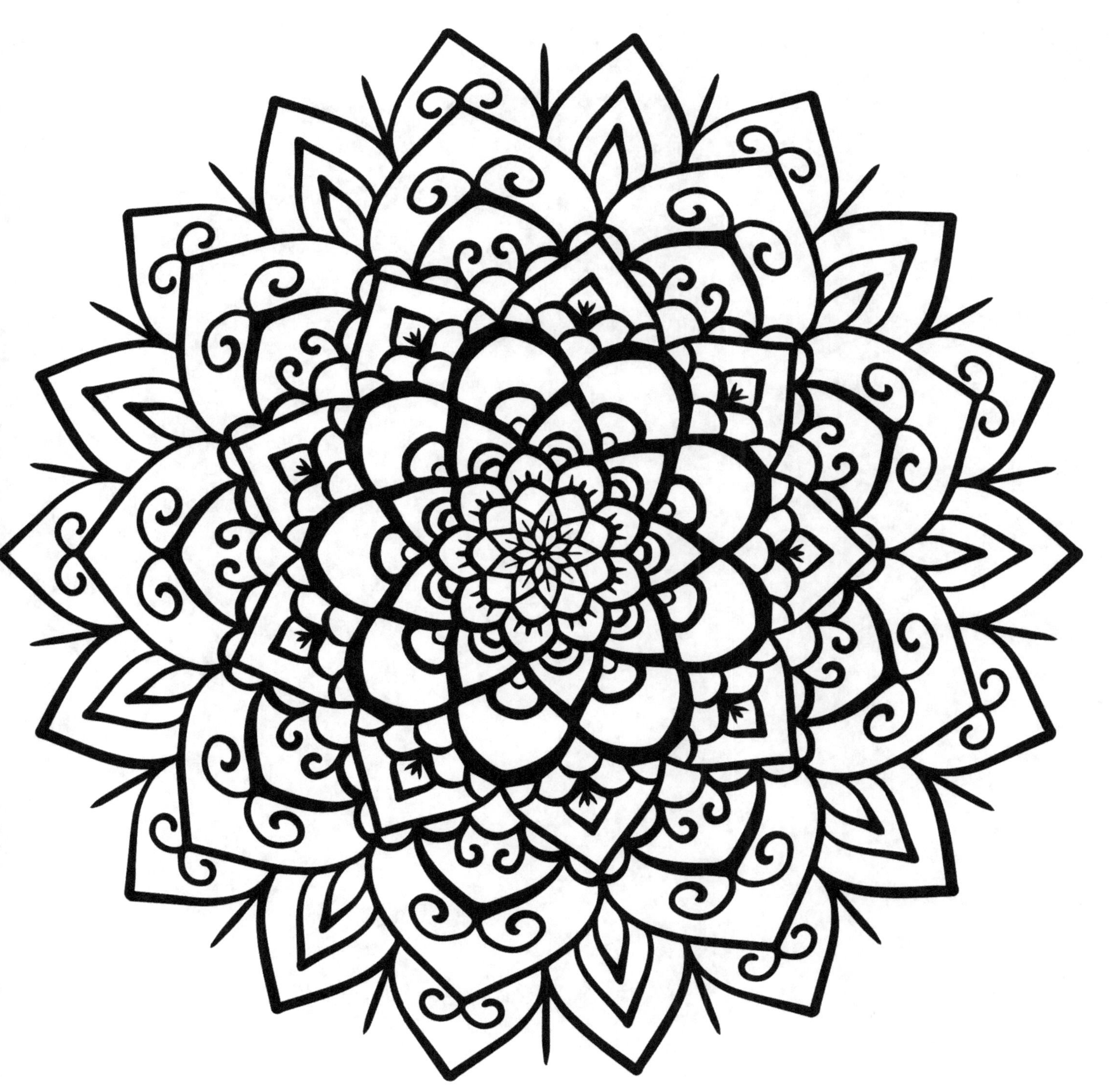

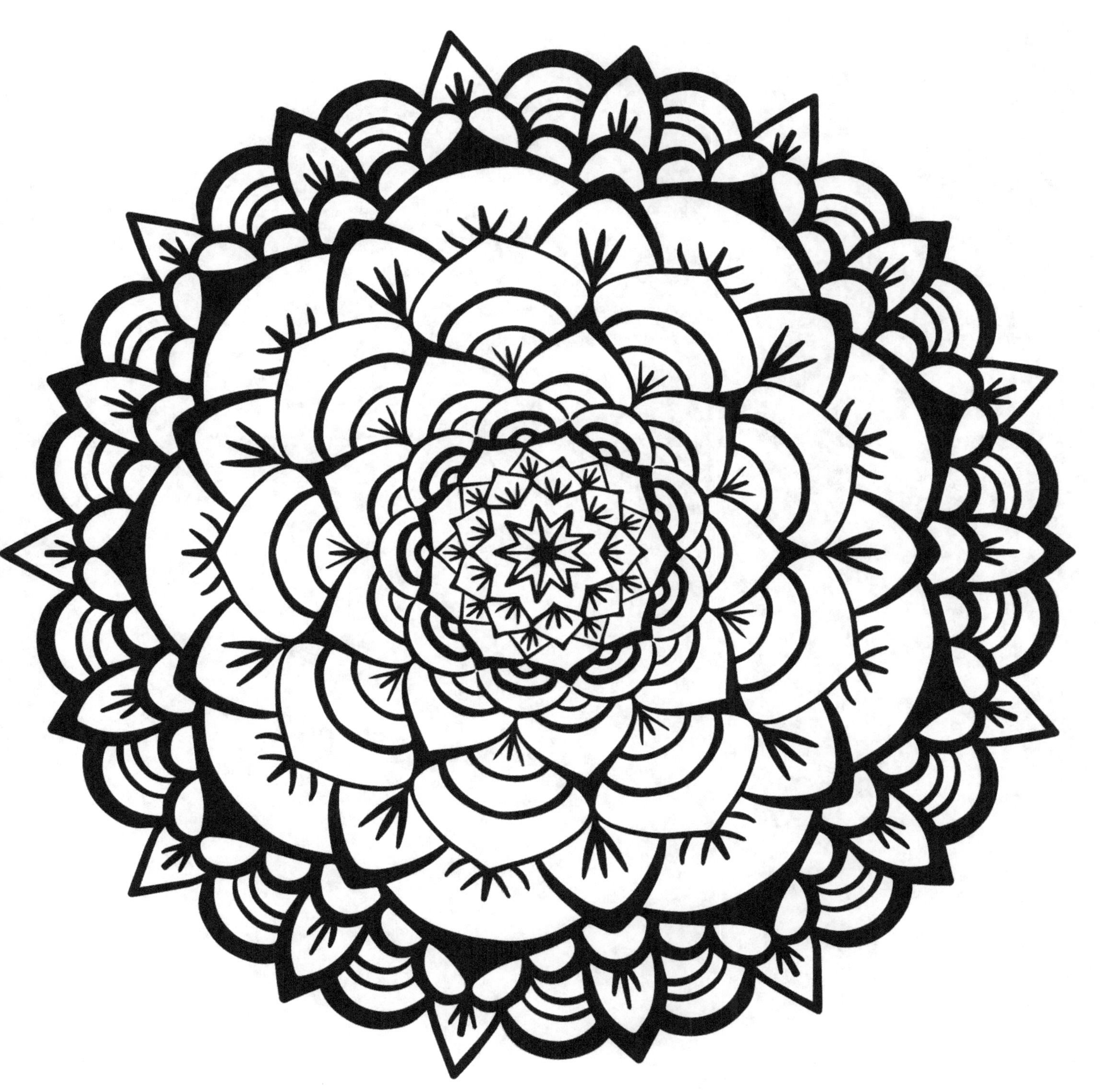

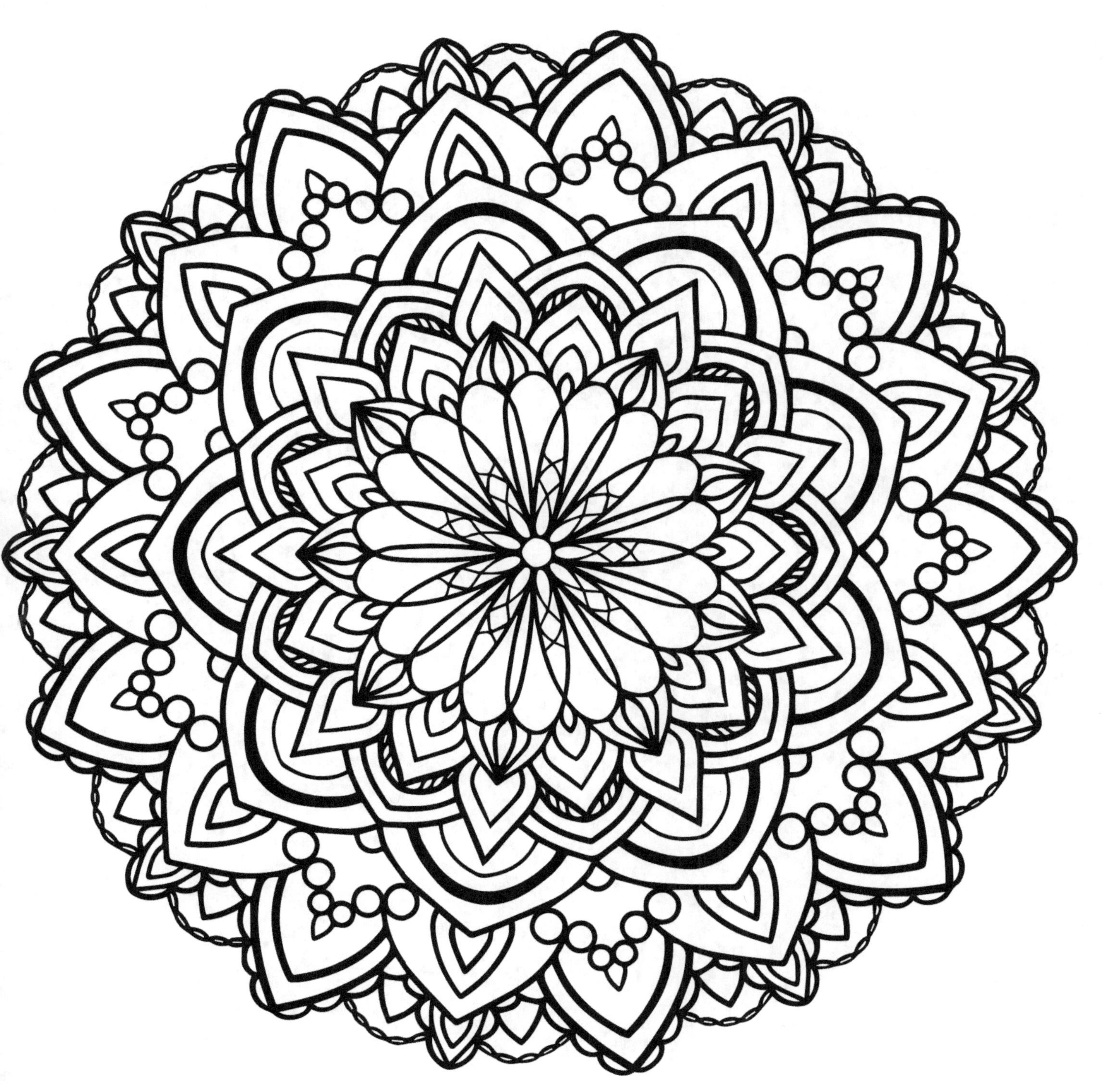

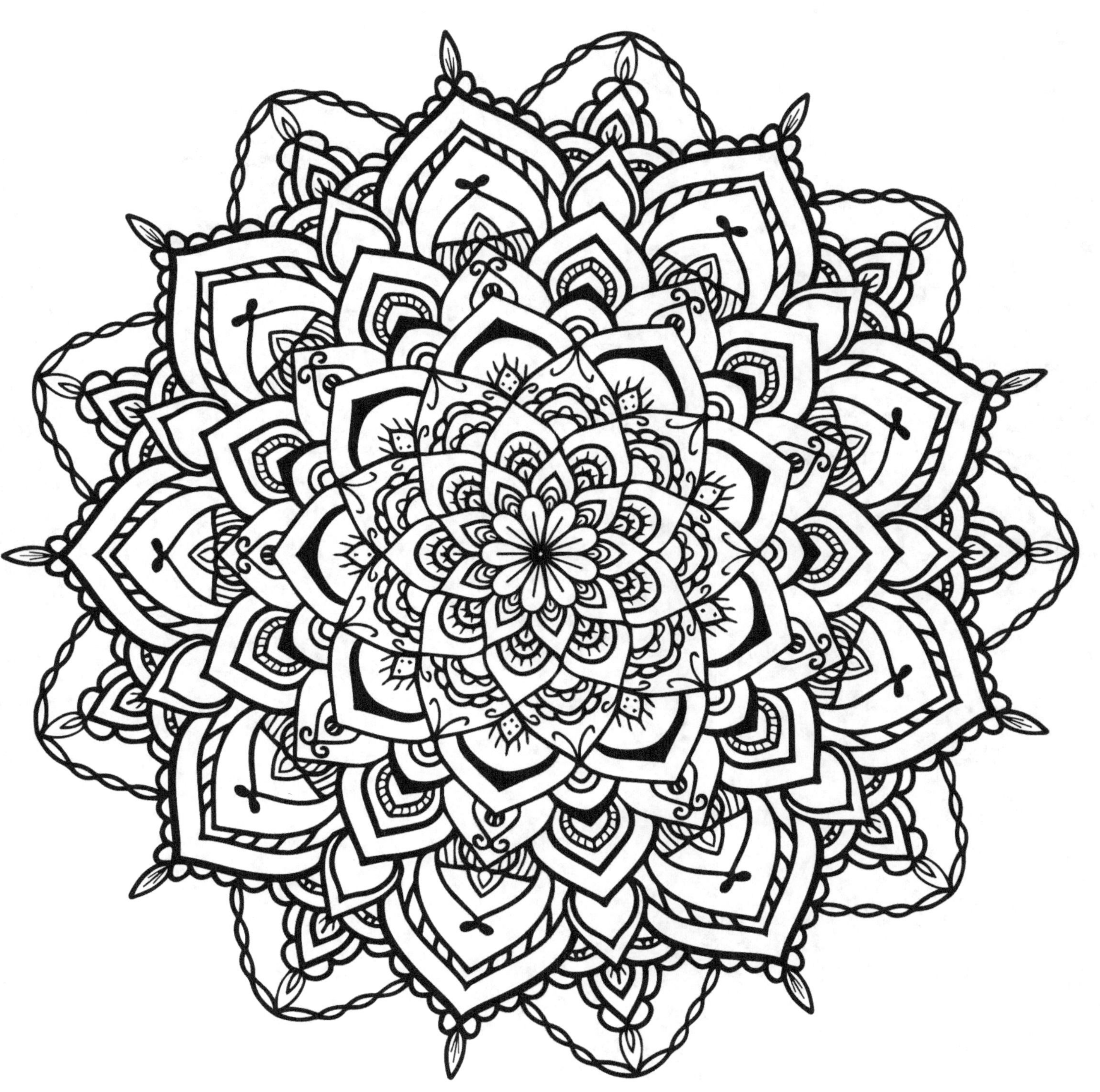

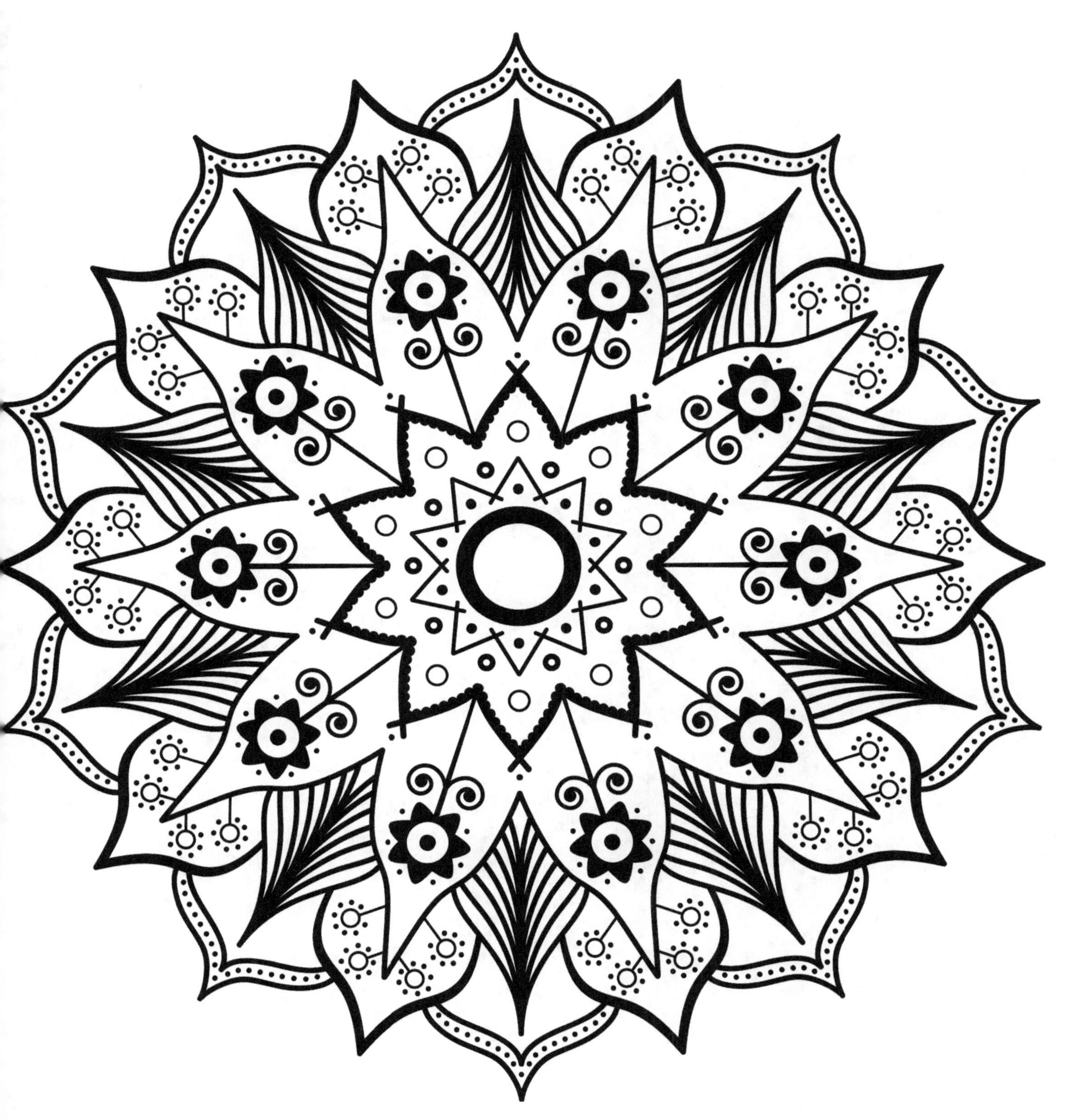

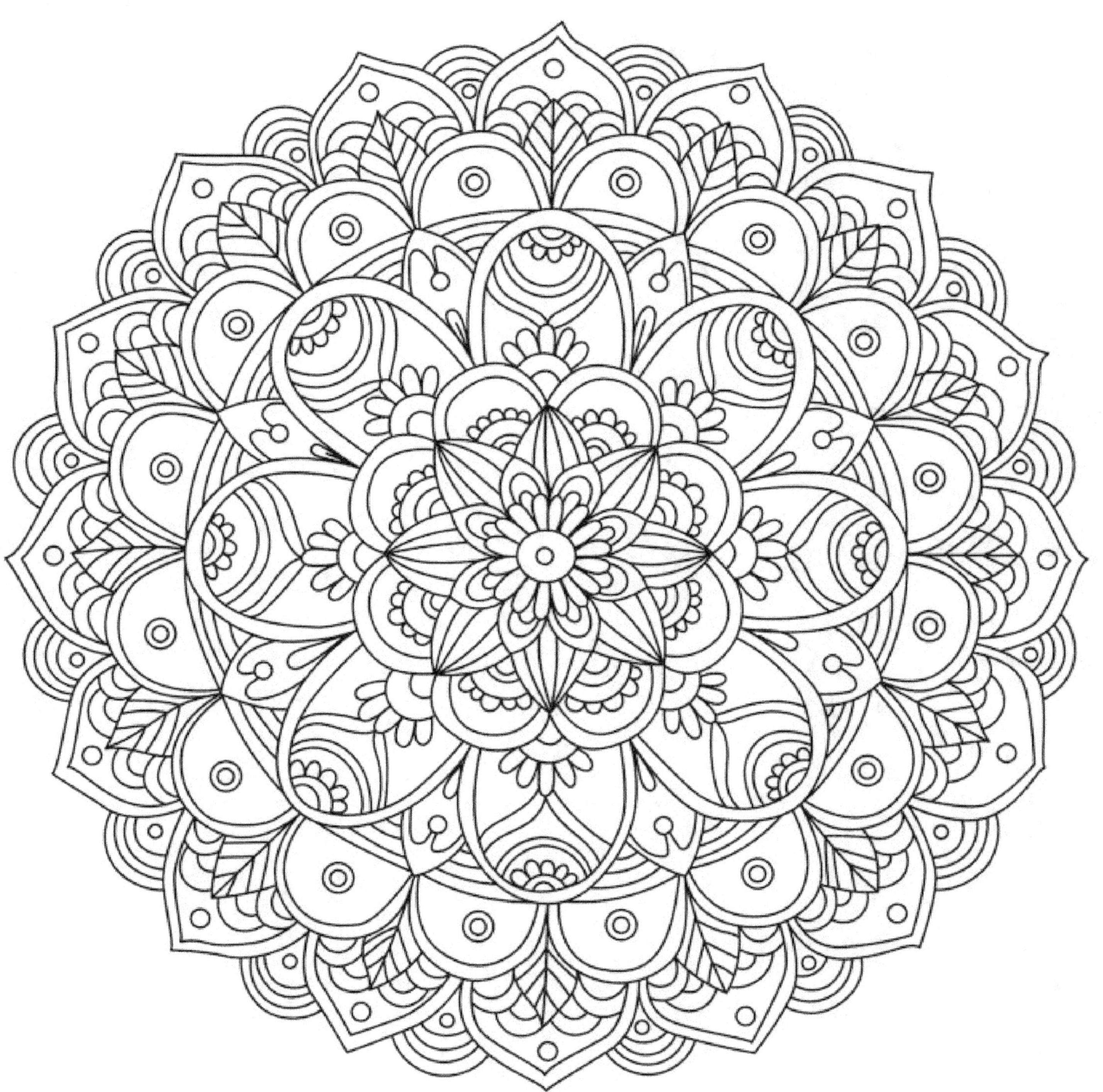

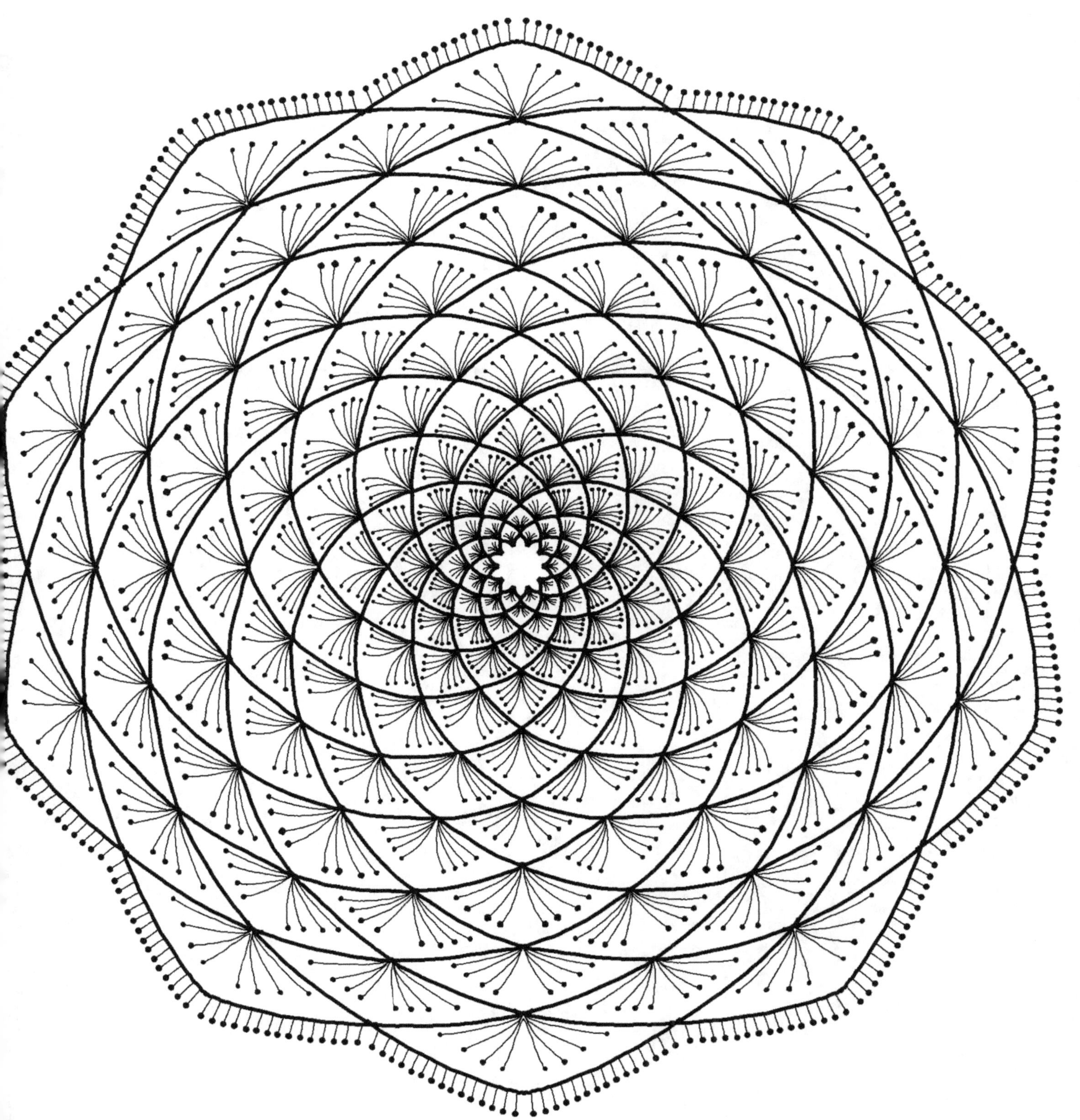

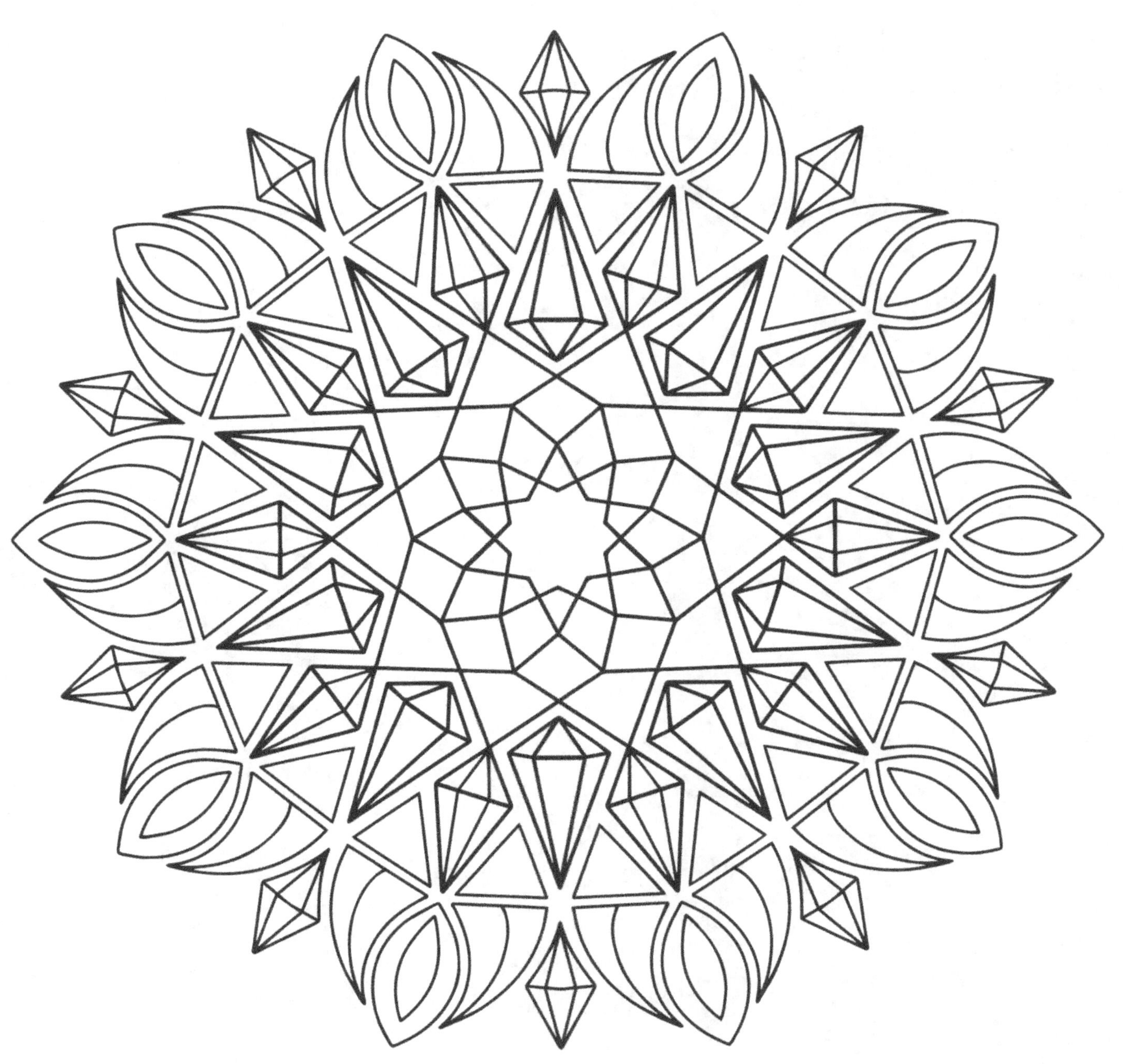

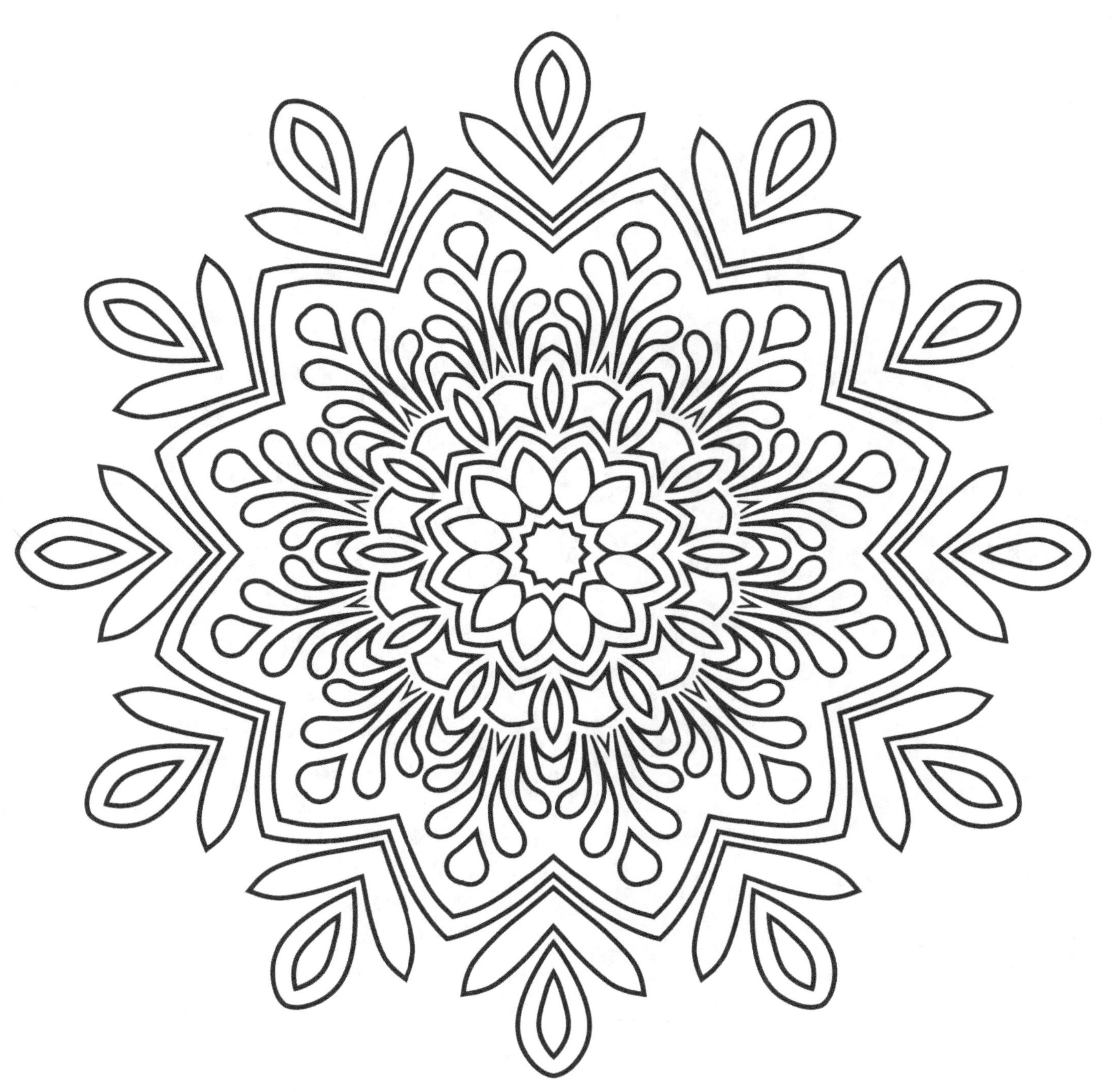

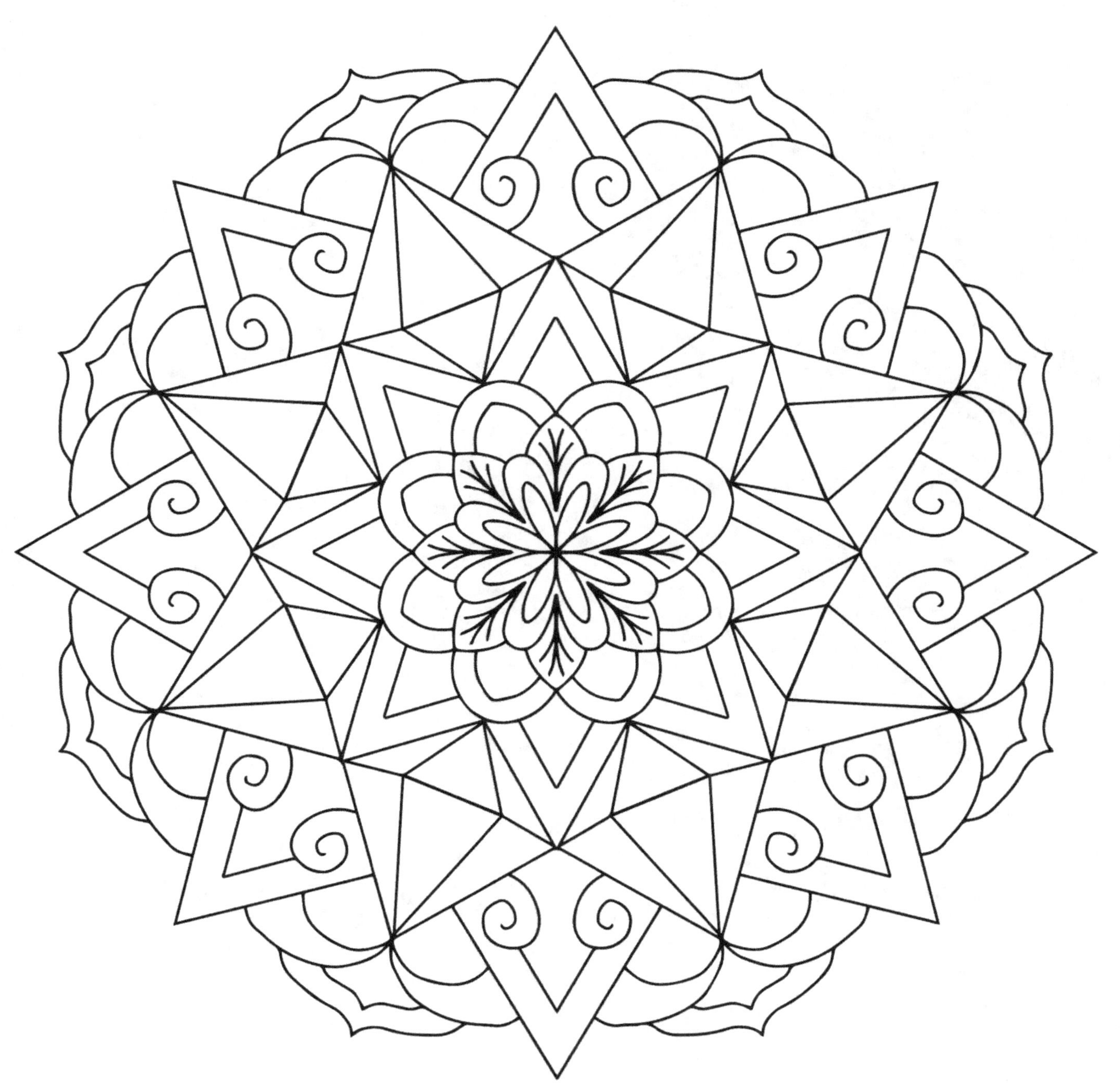

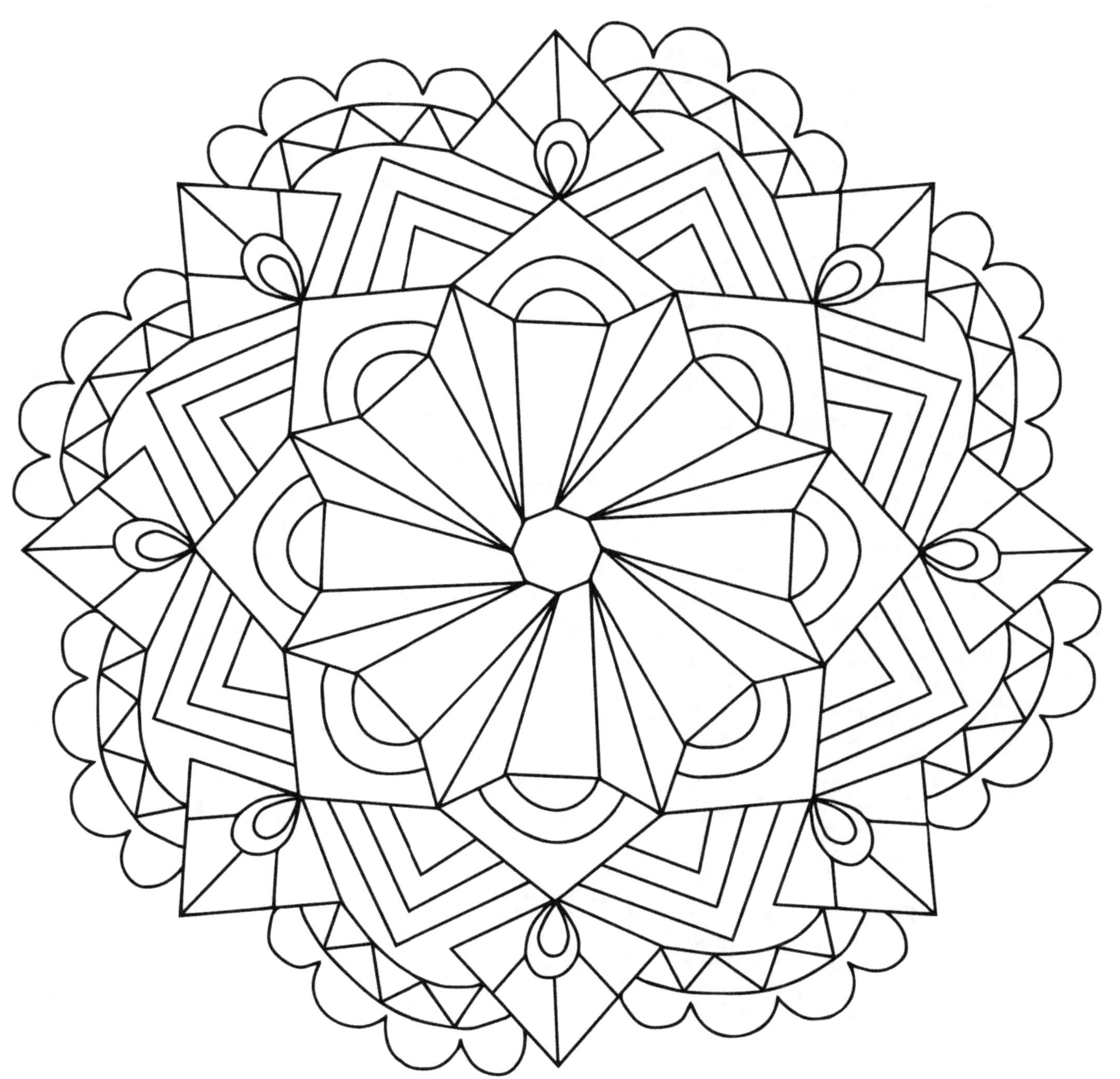

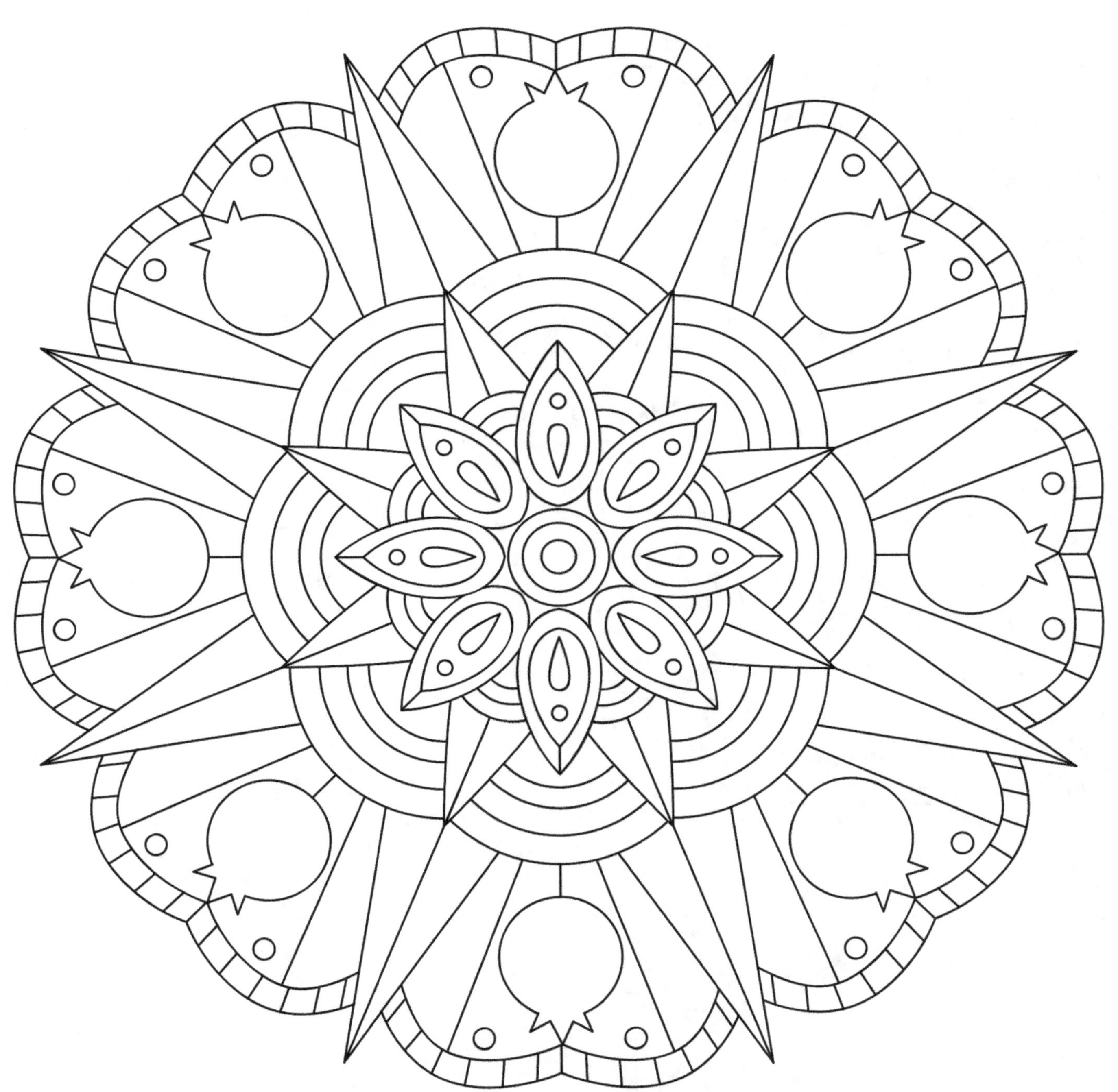

MODERATE

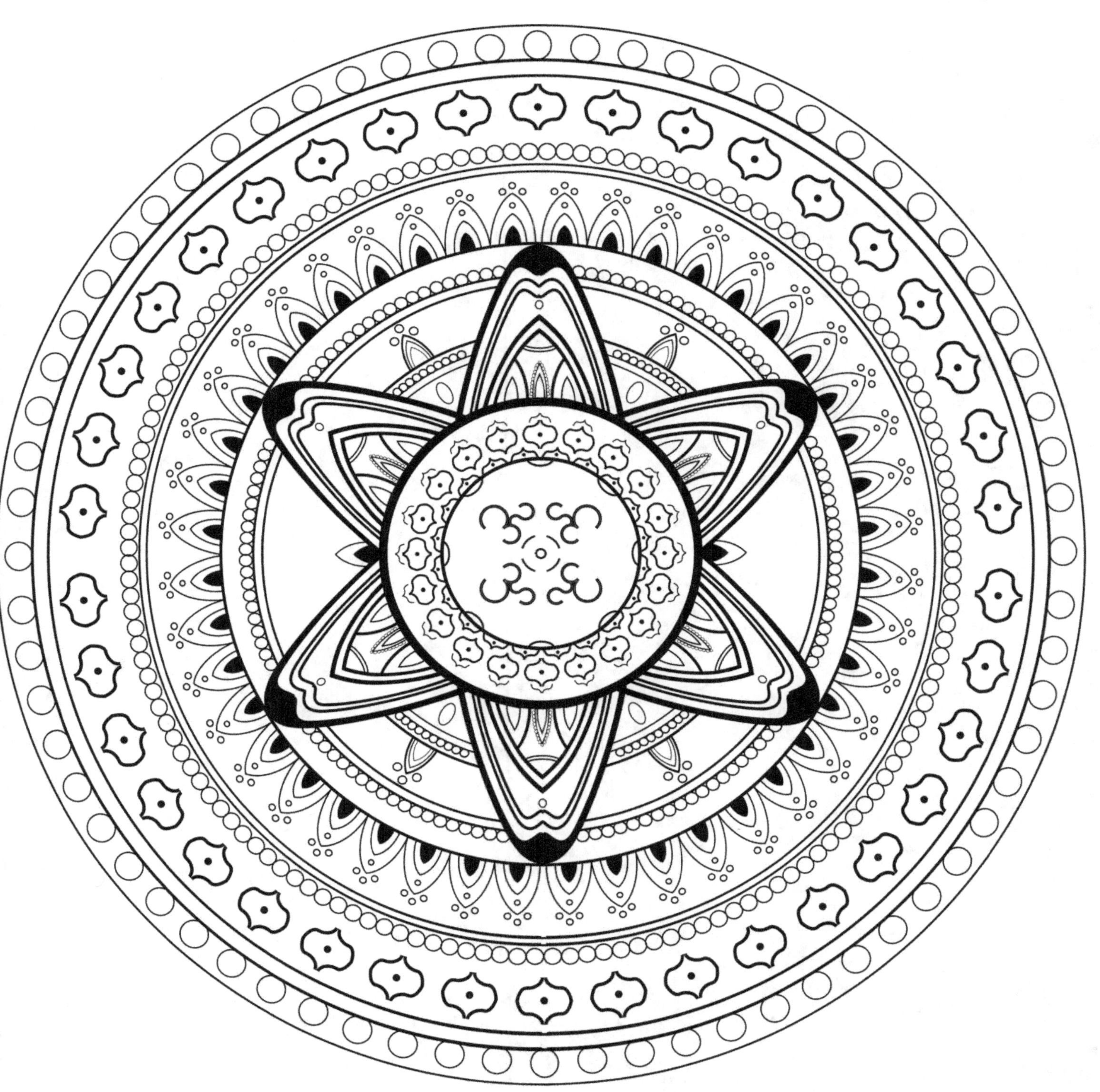

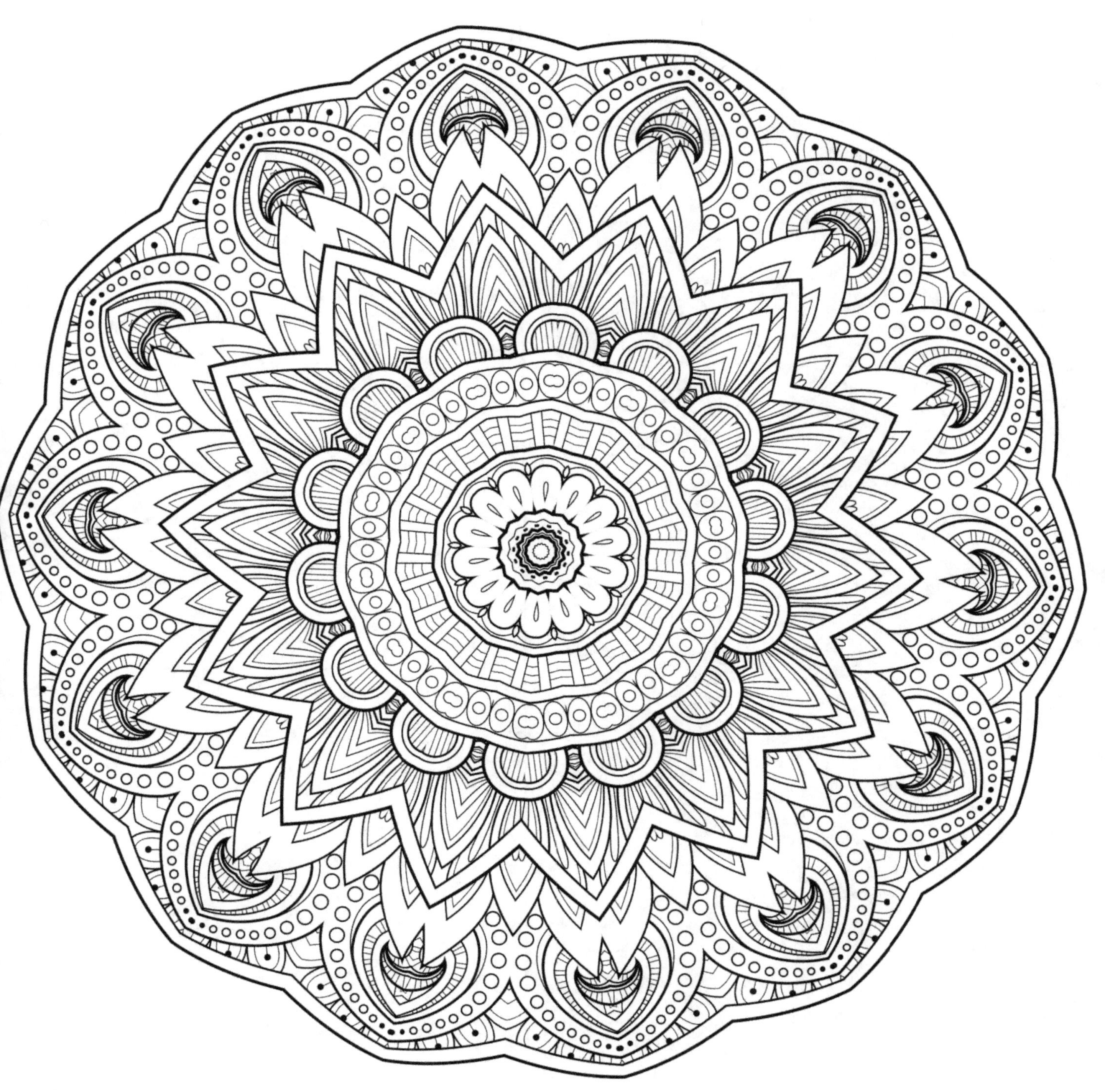

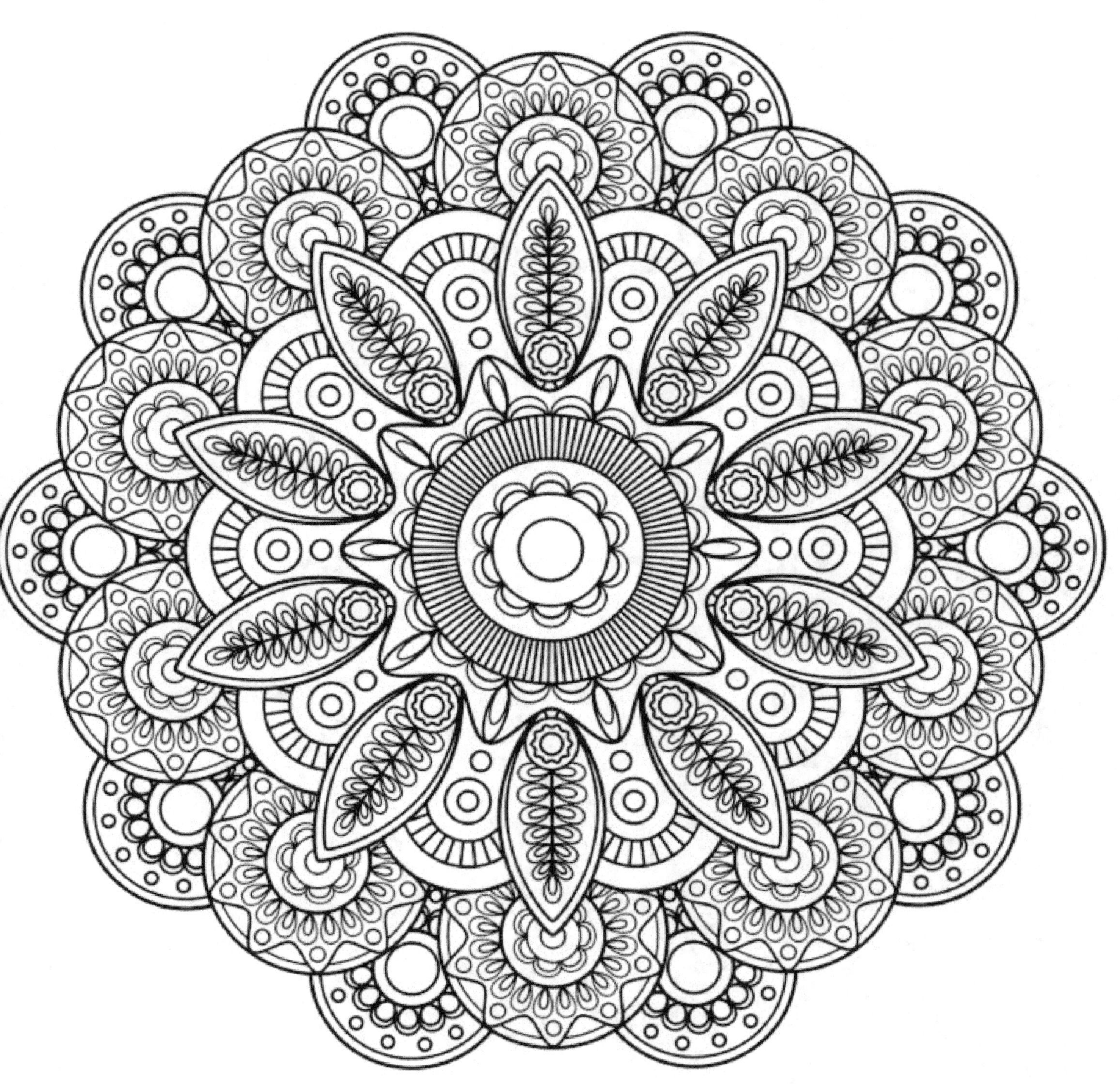

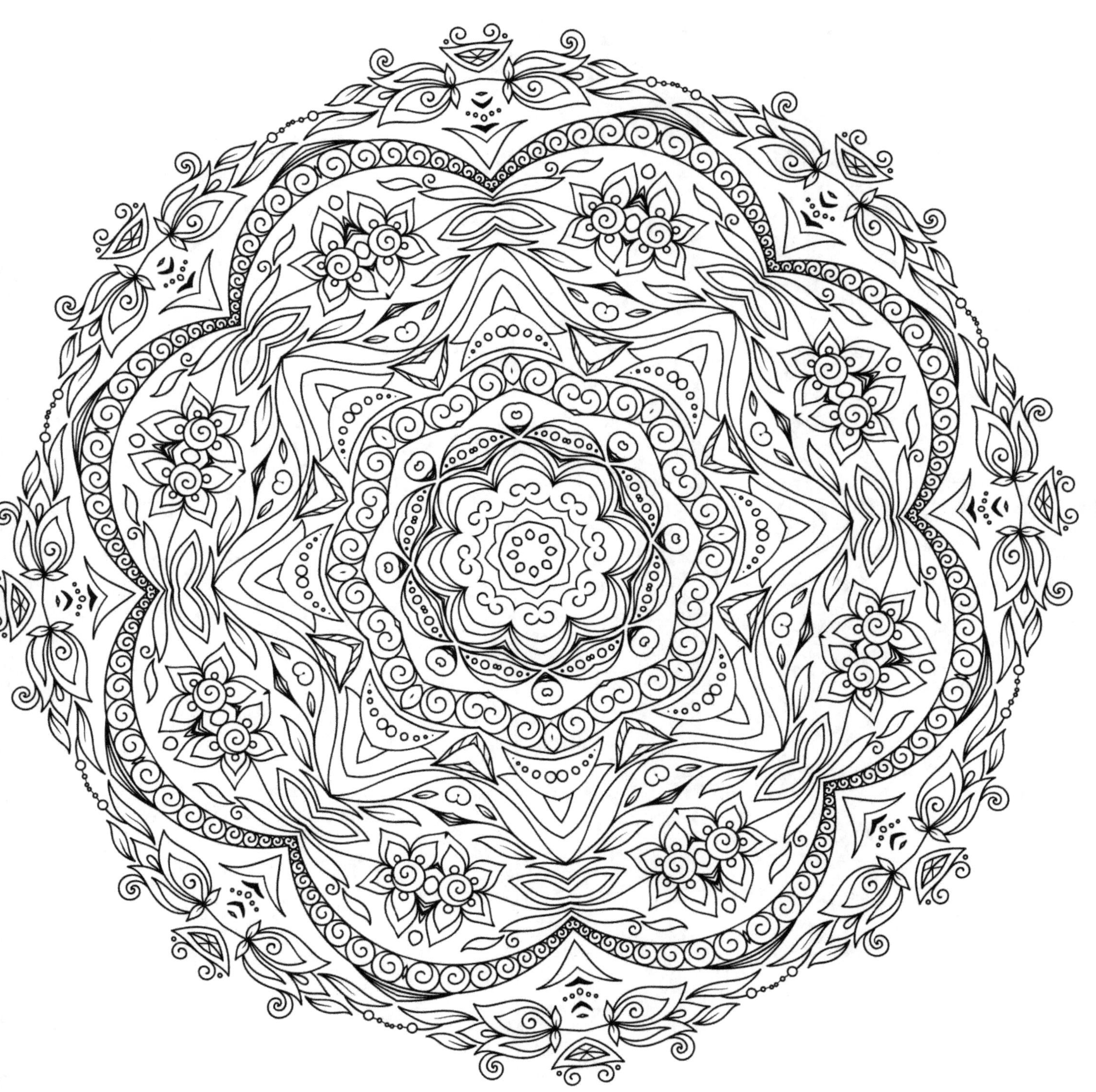

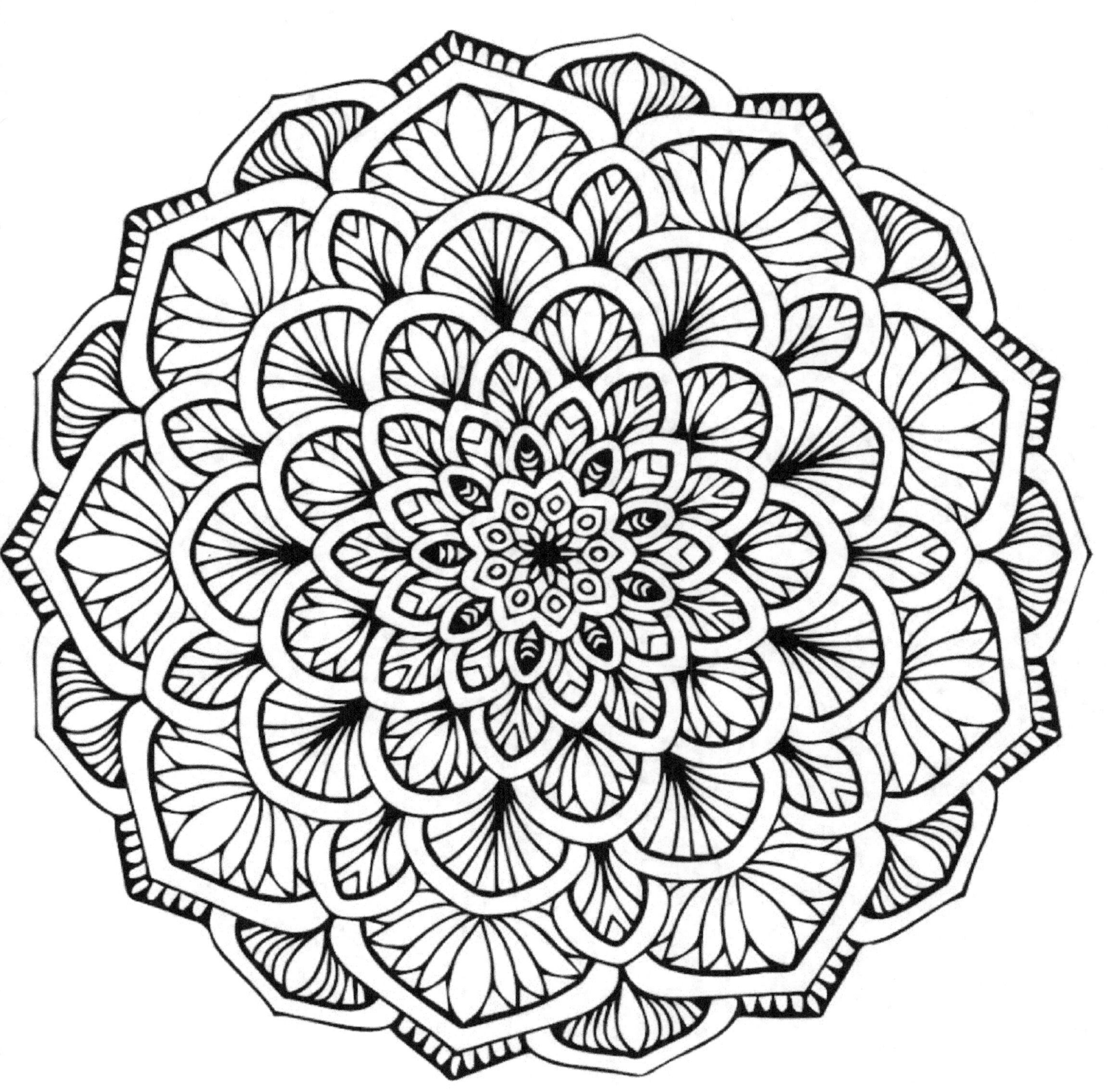

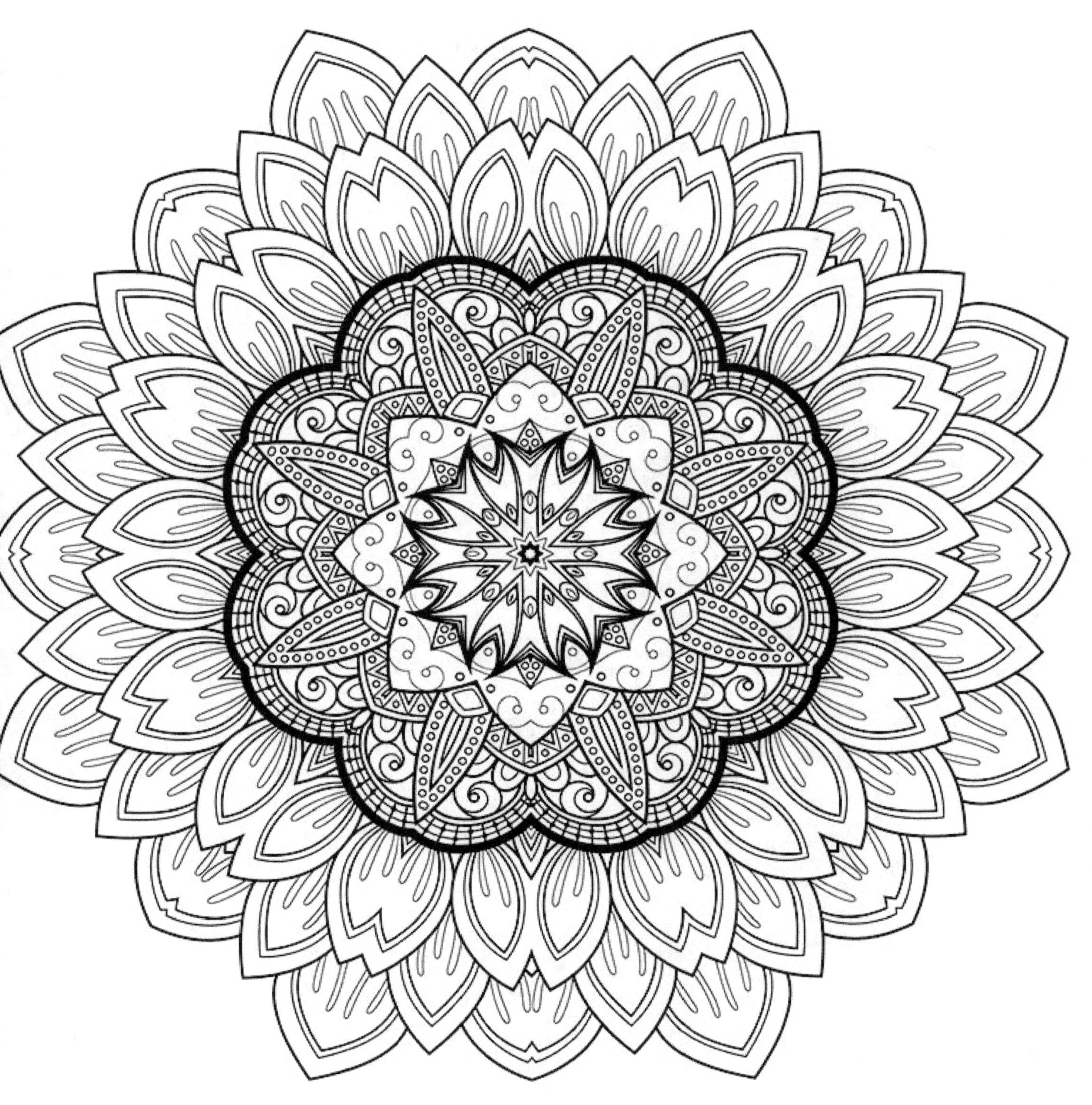

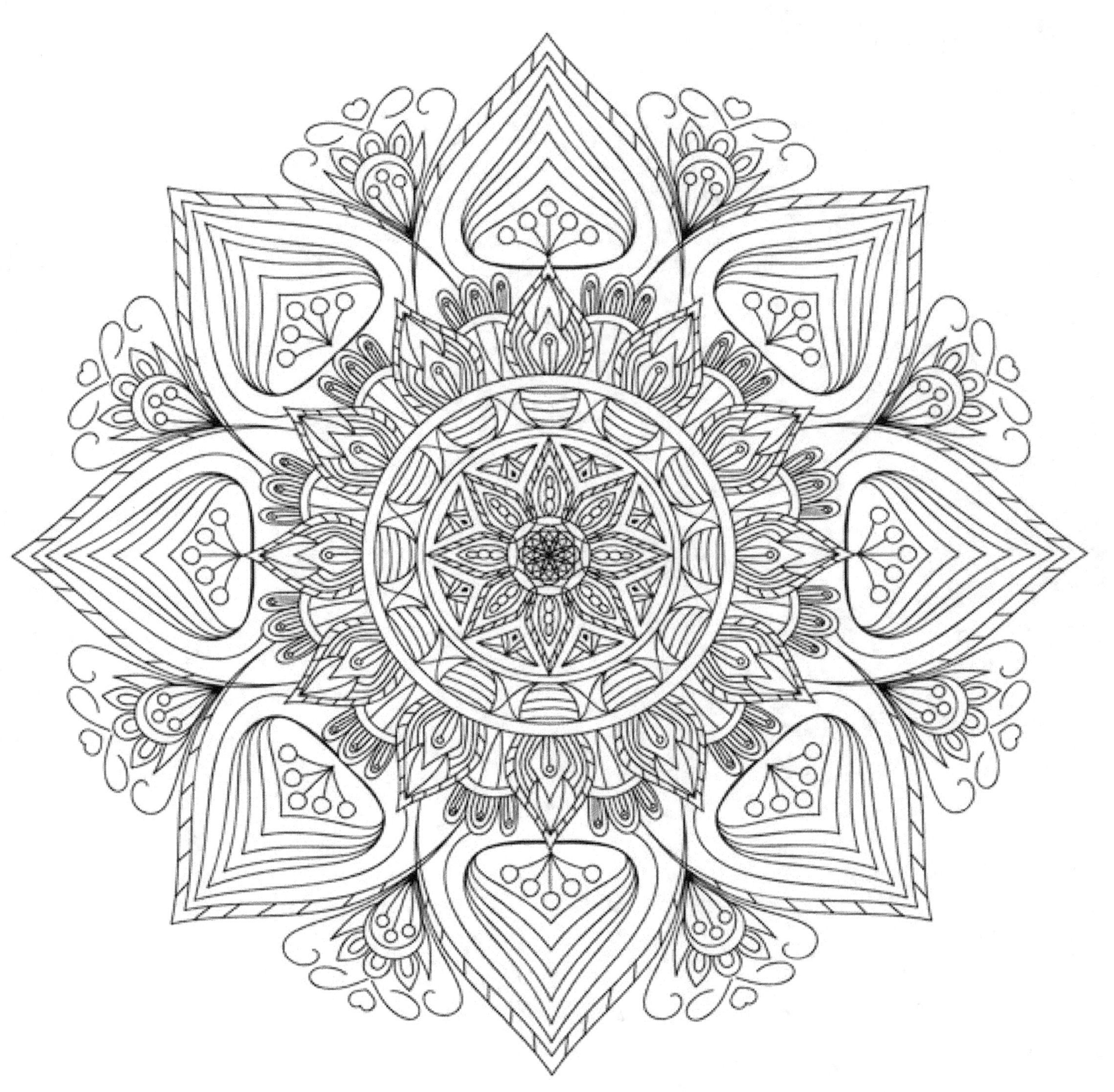

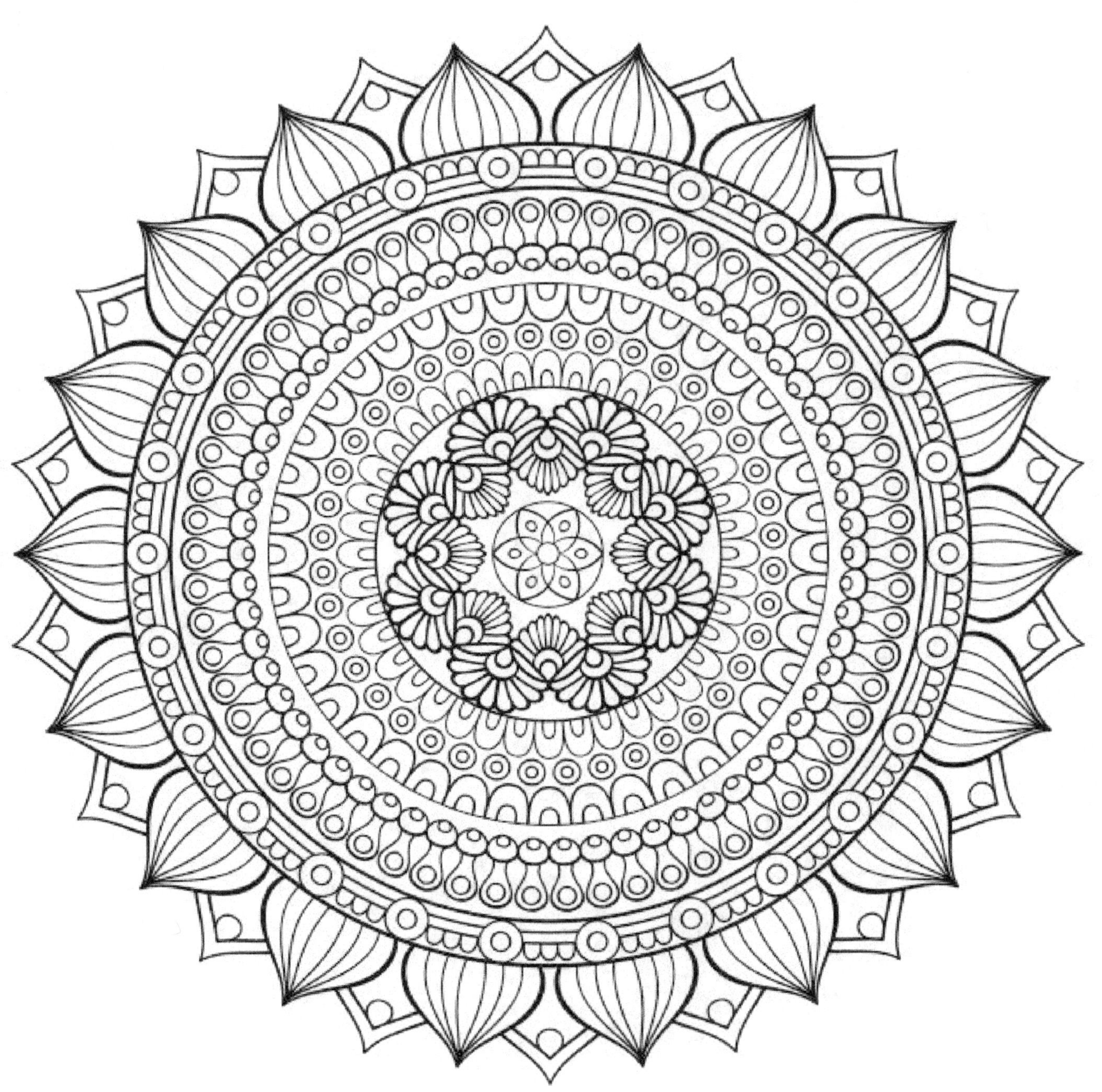

ADVANCE

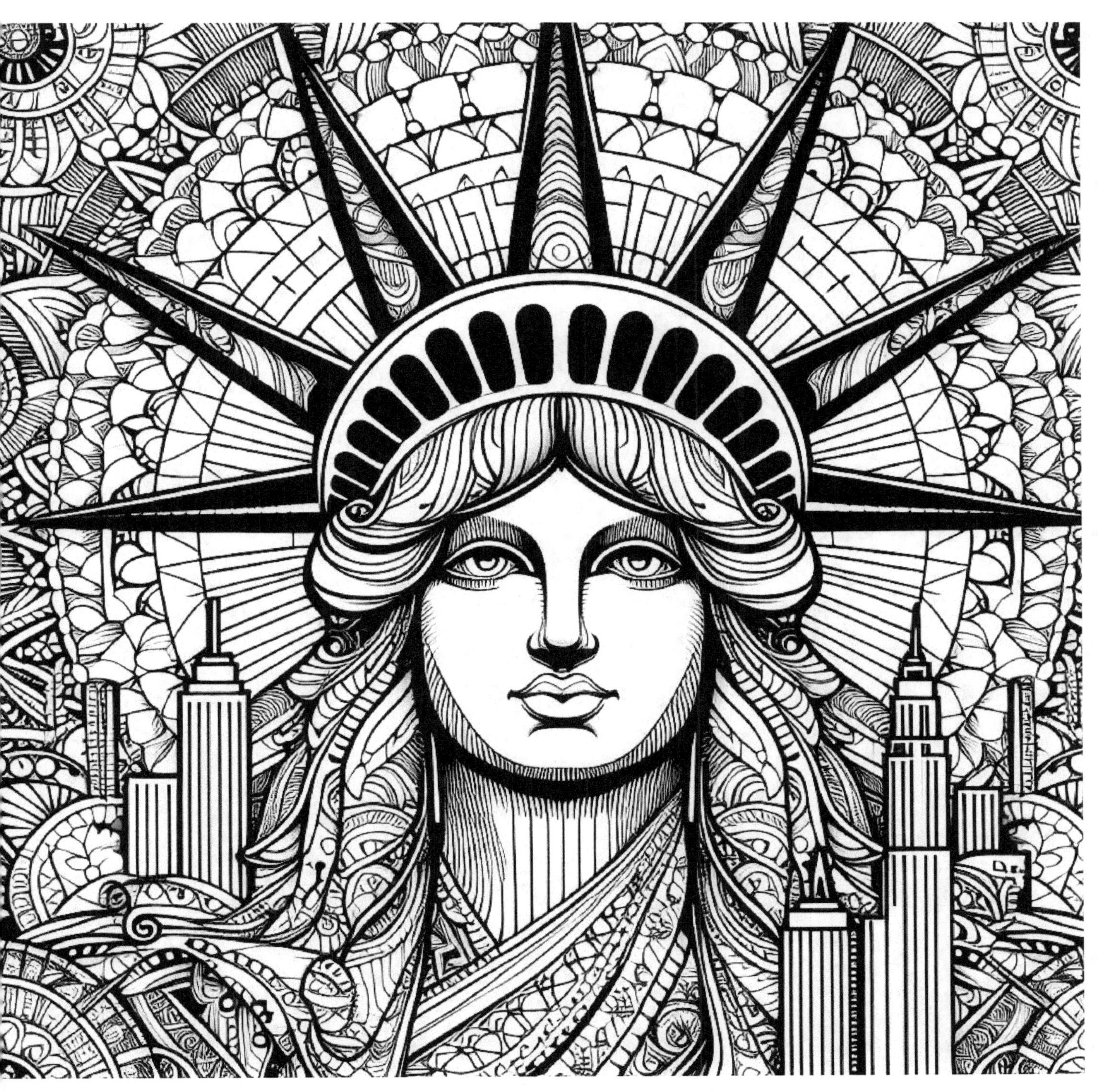

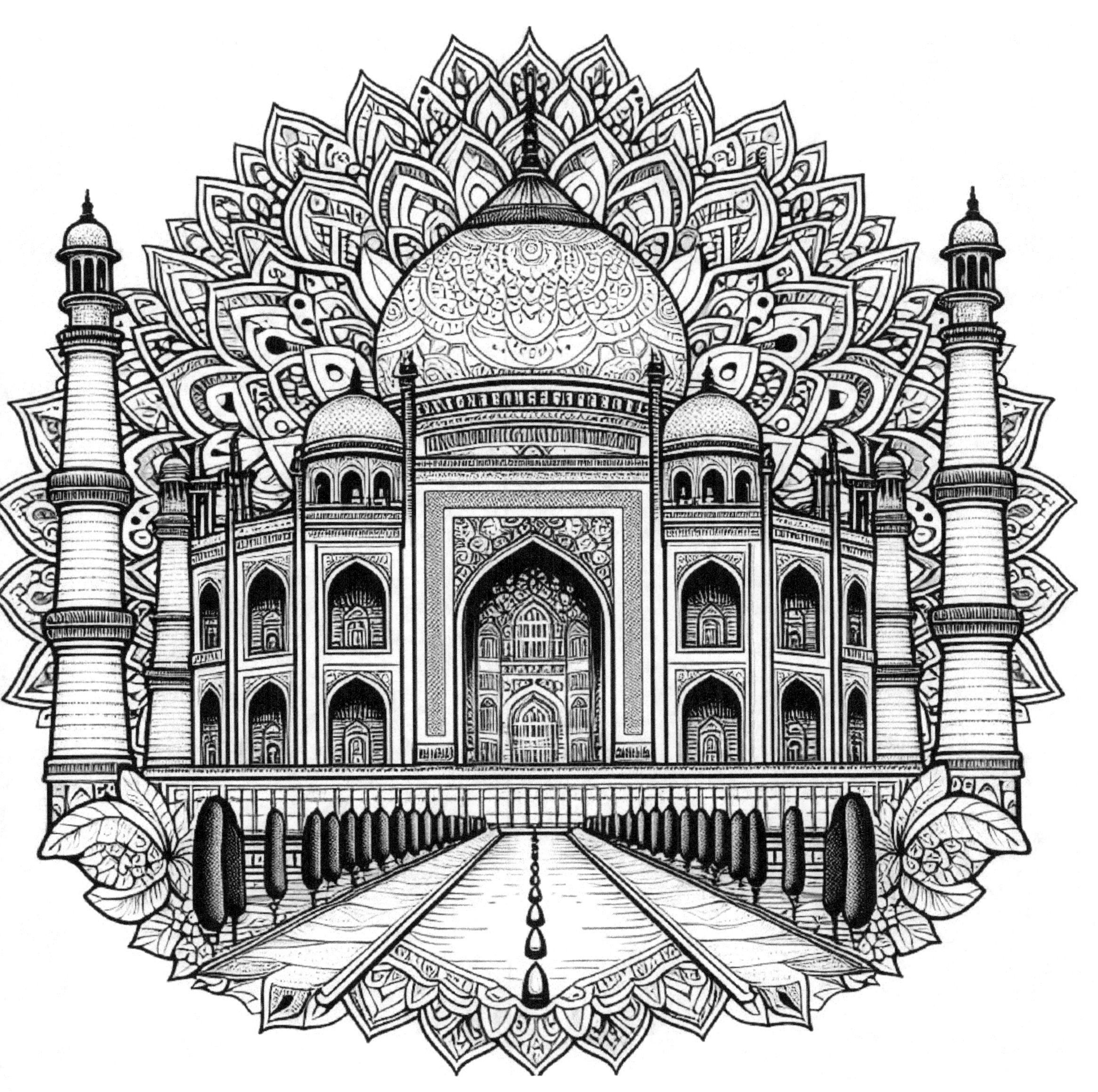

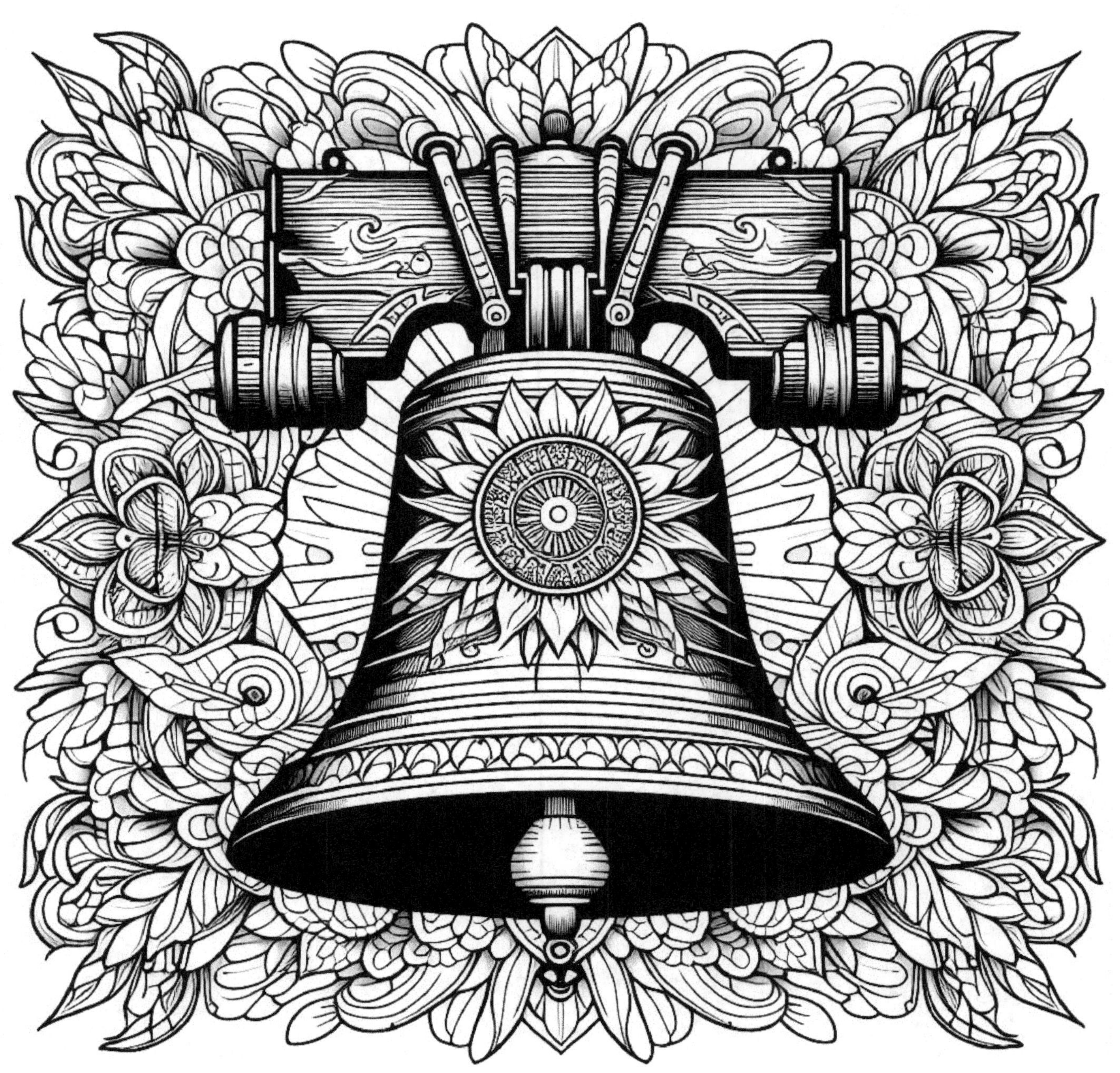

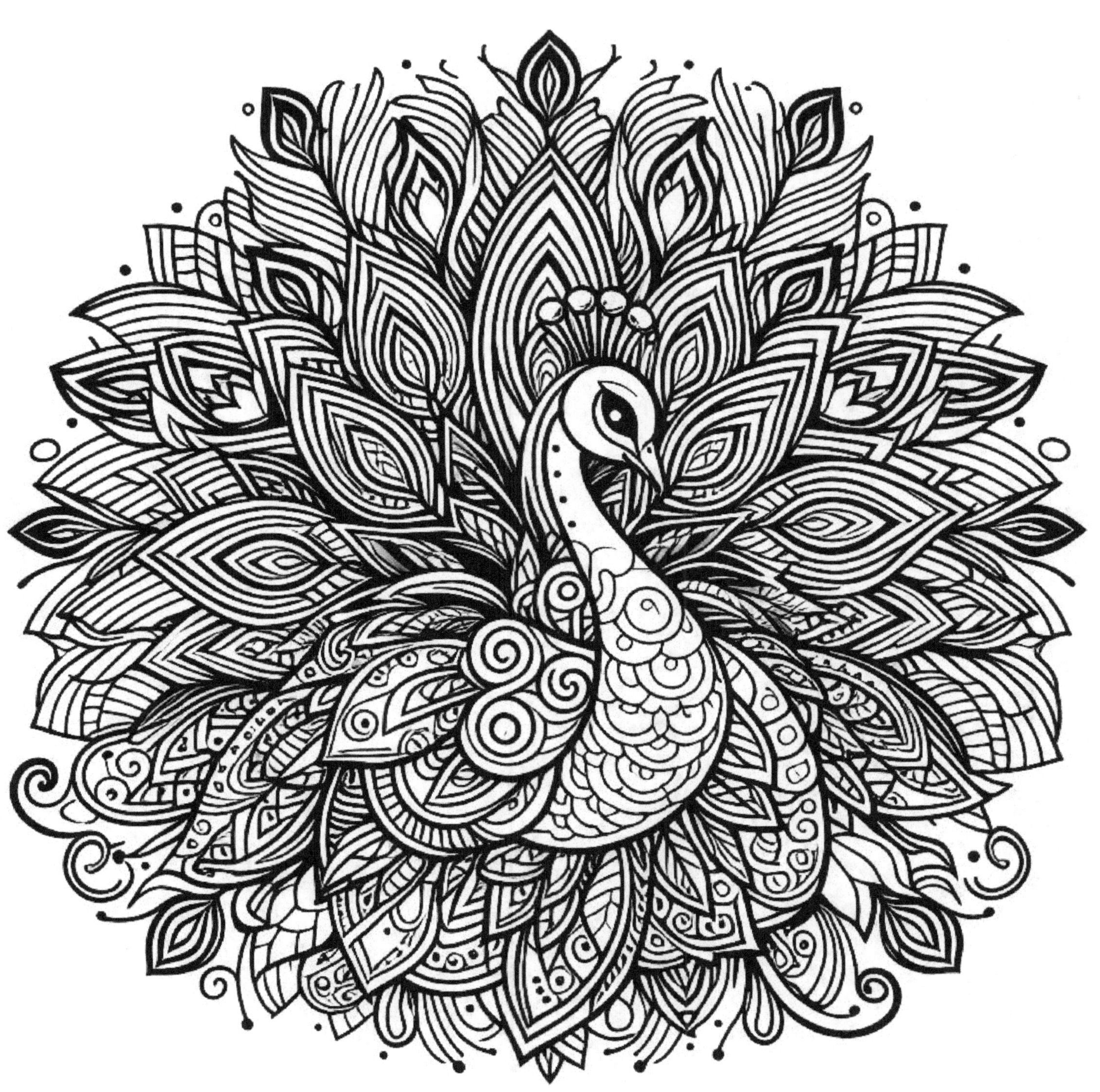

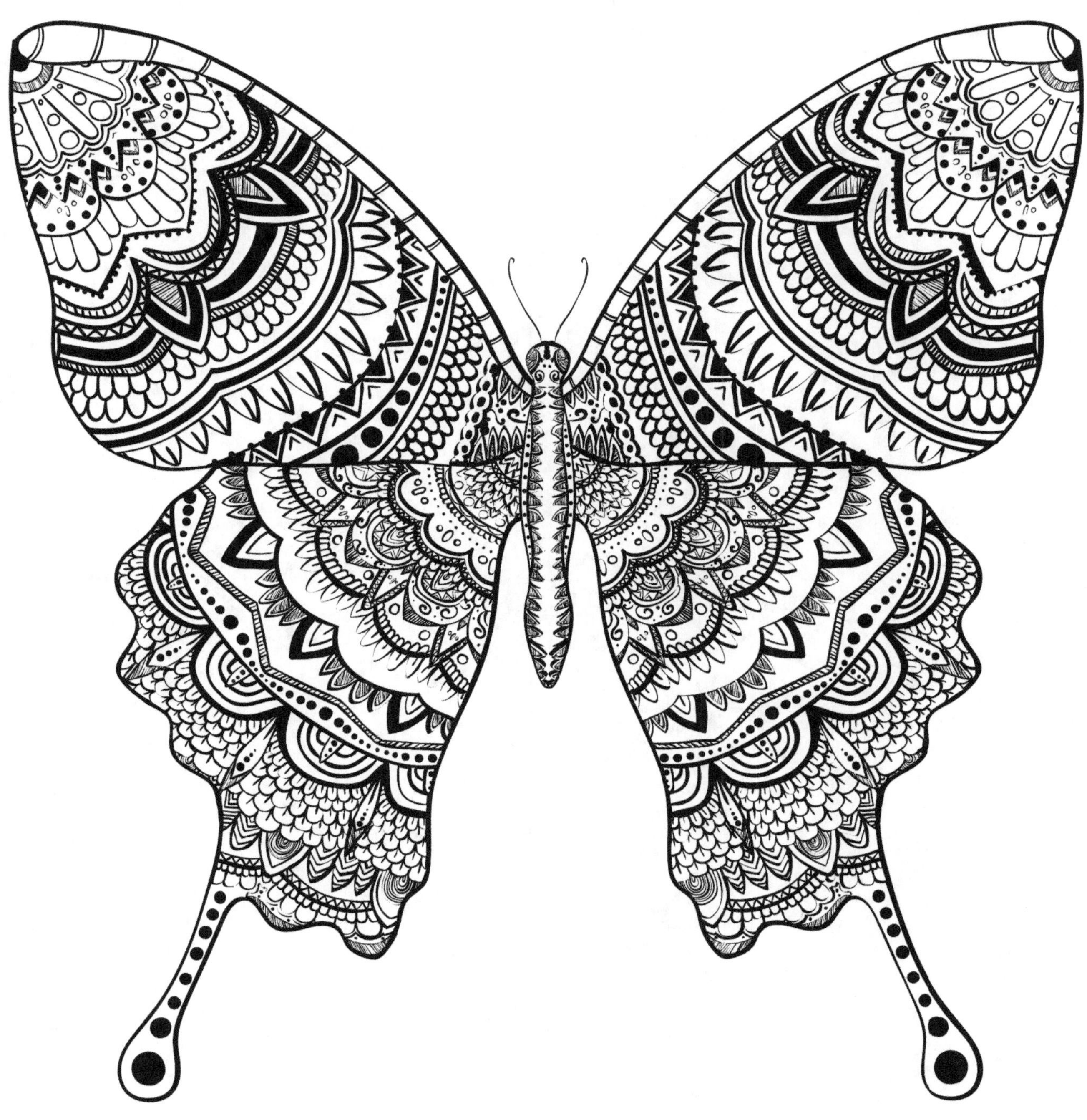

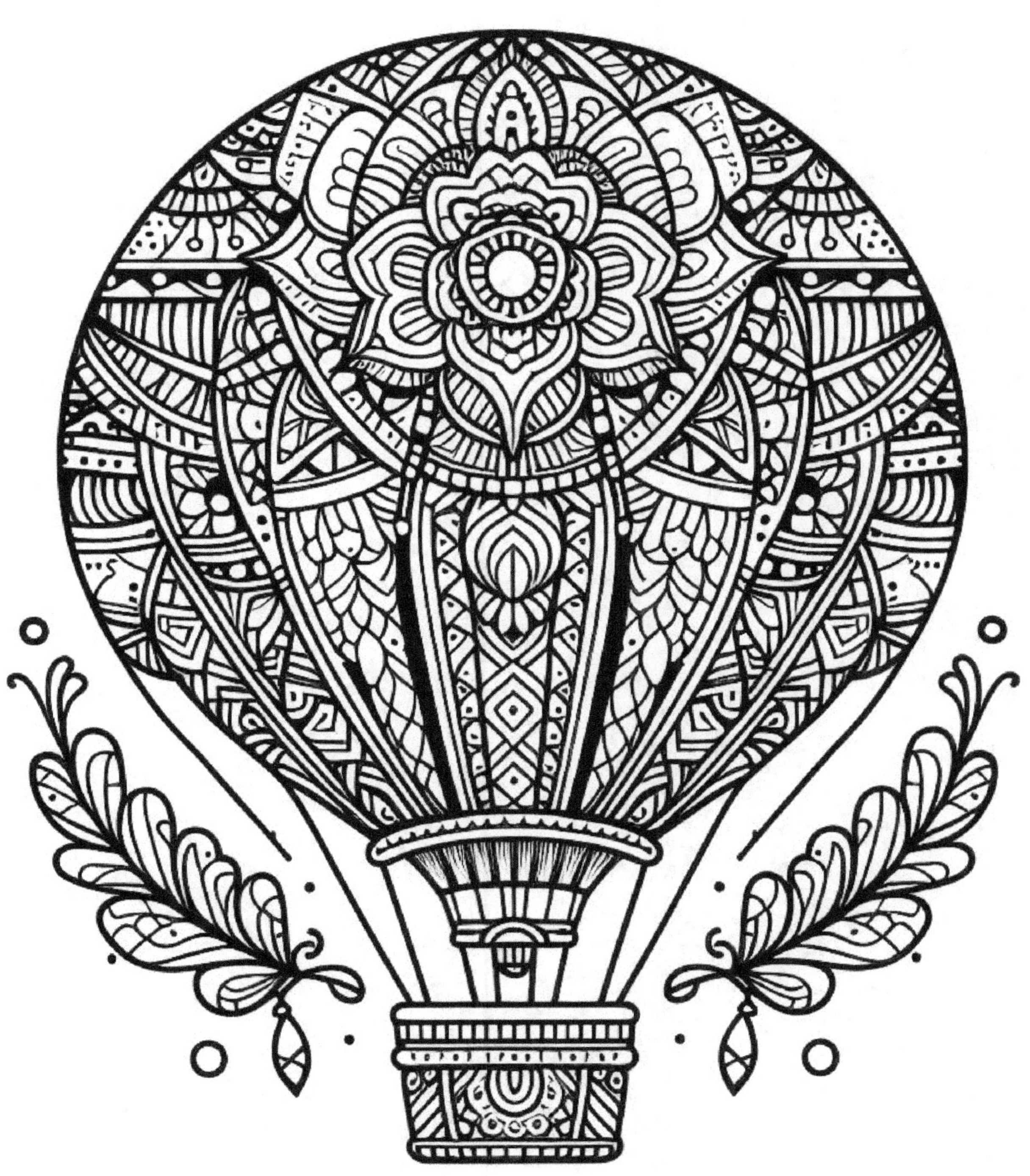

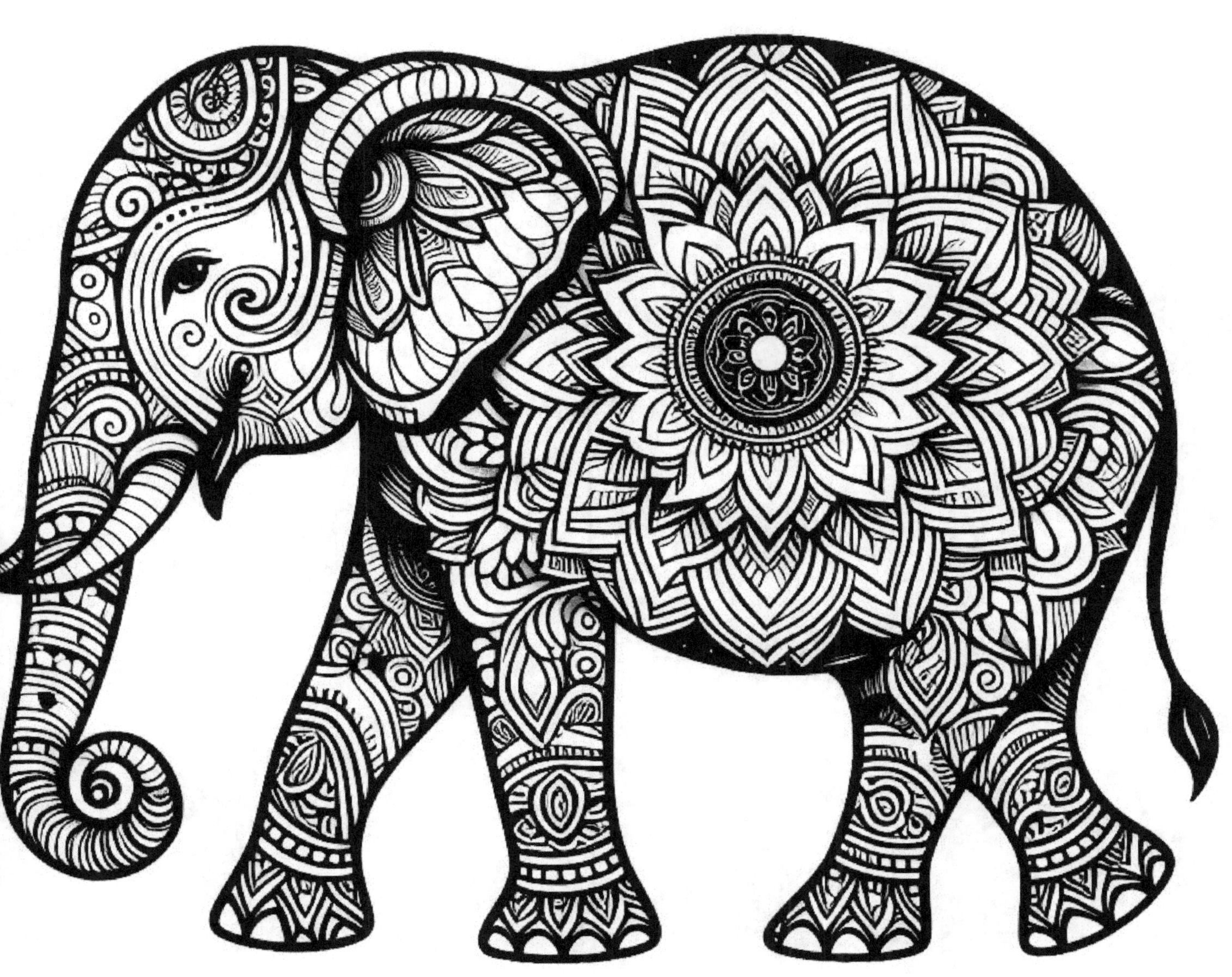

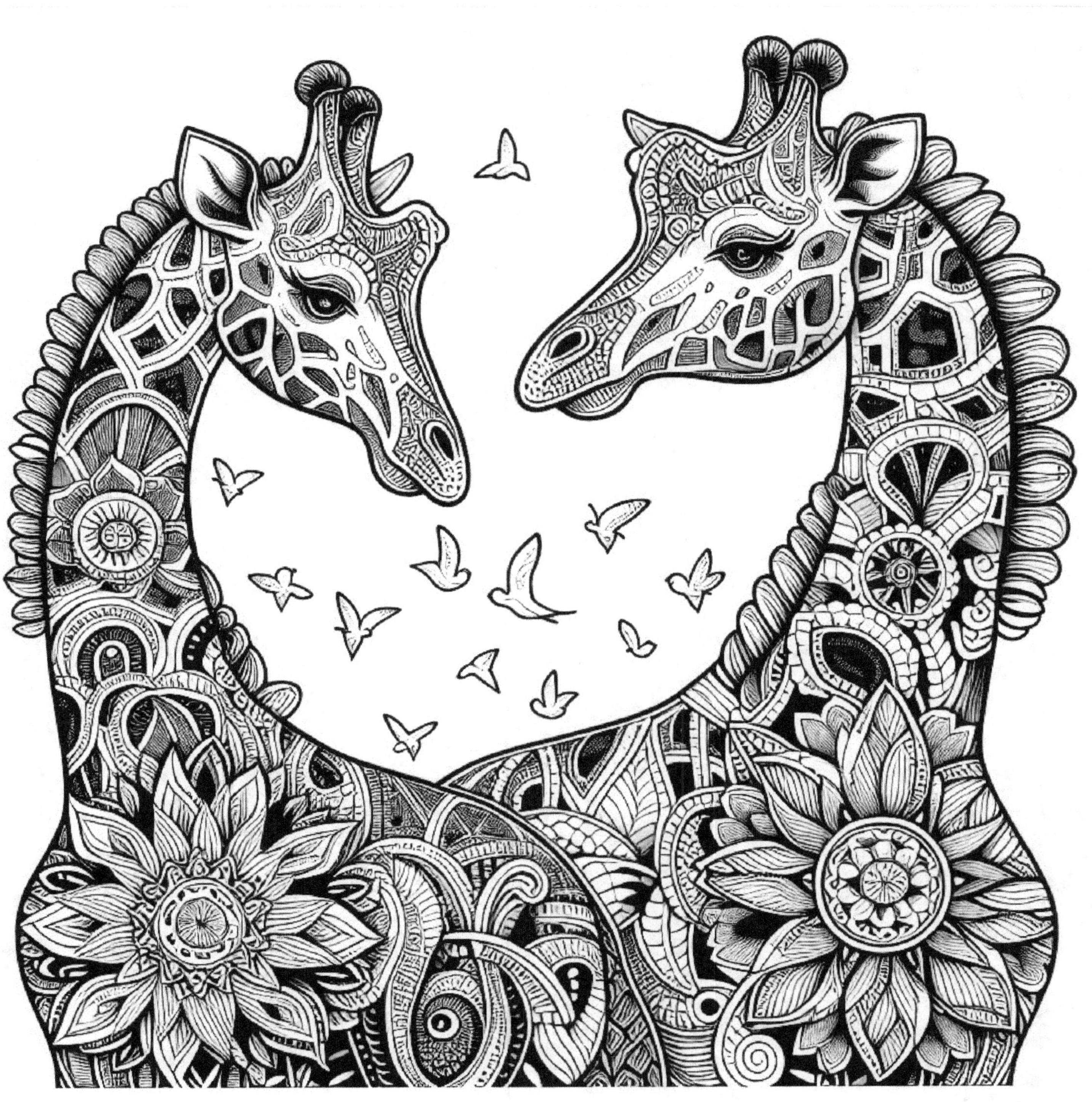

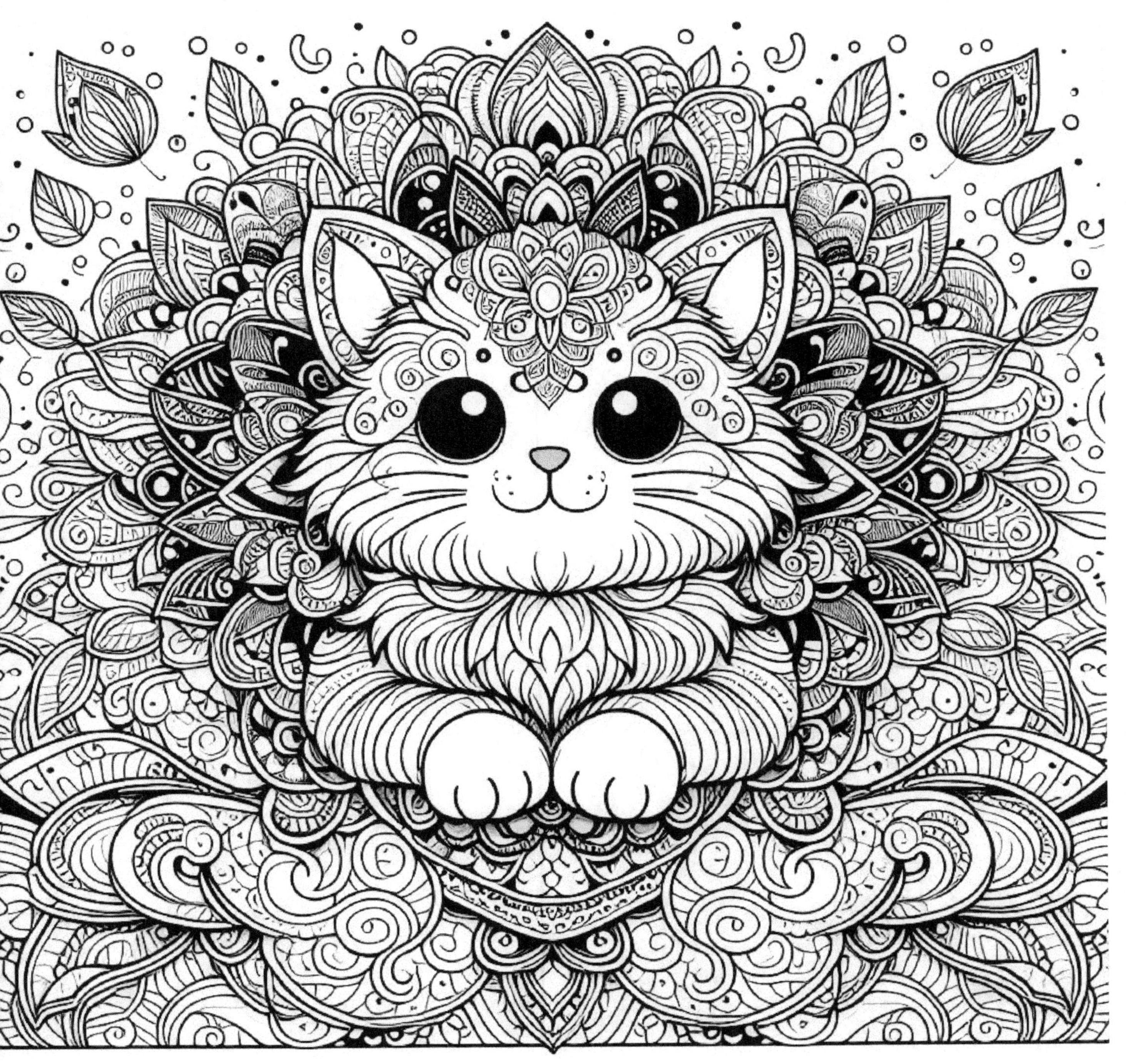

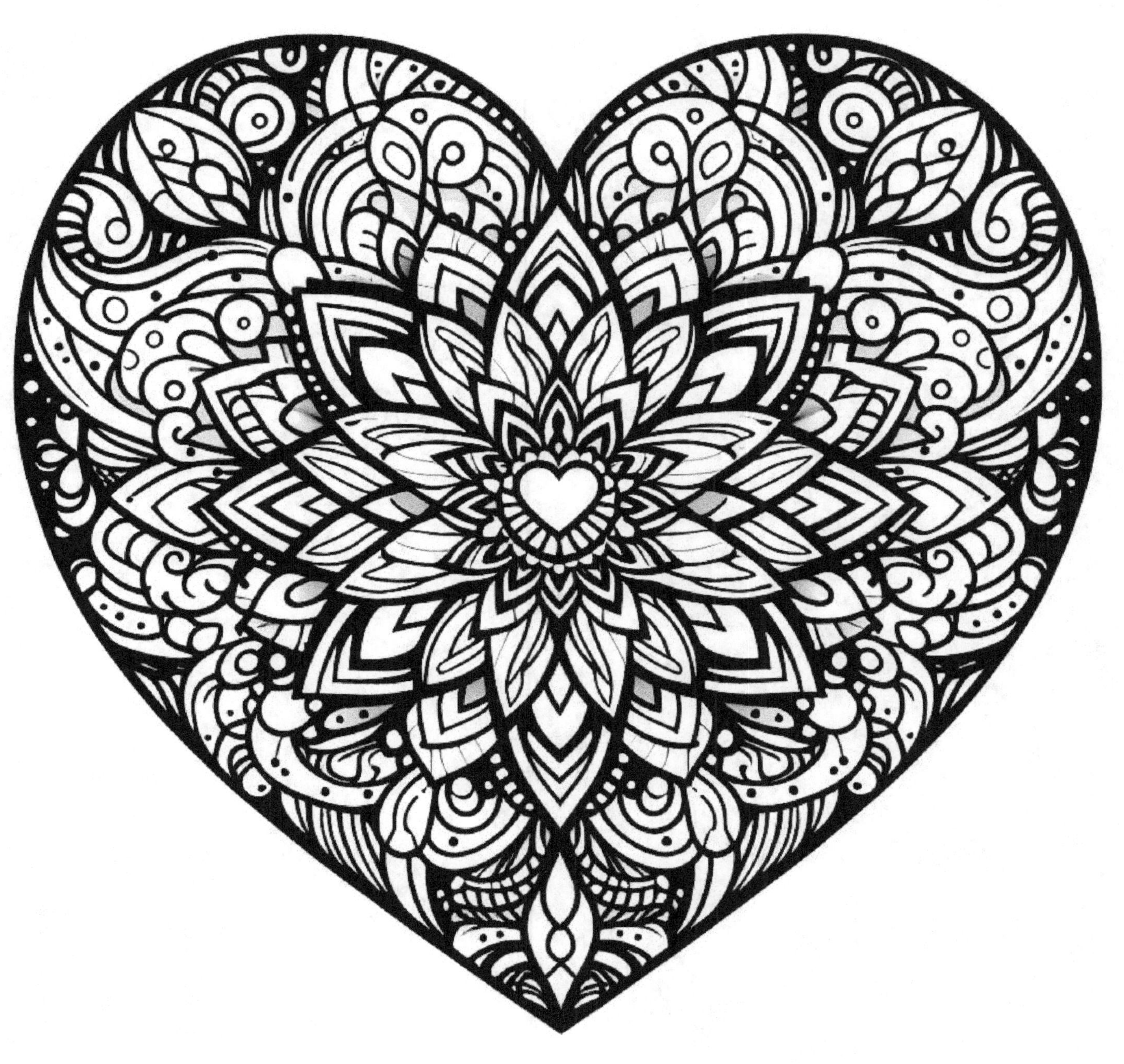

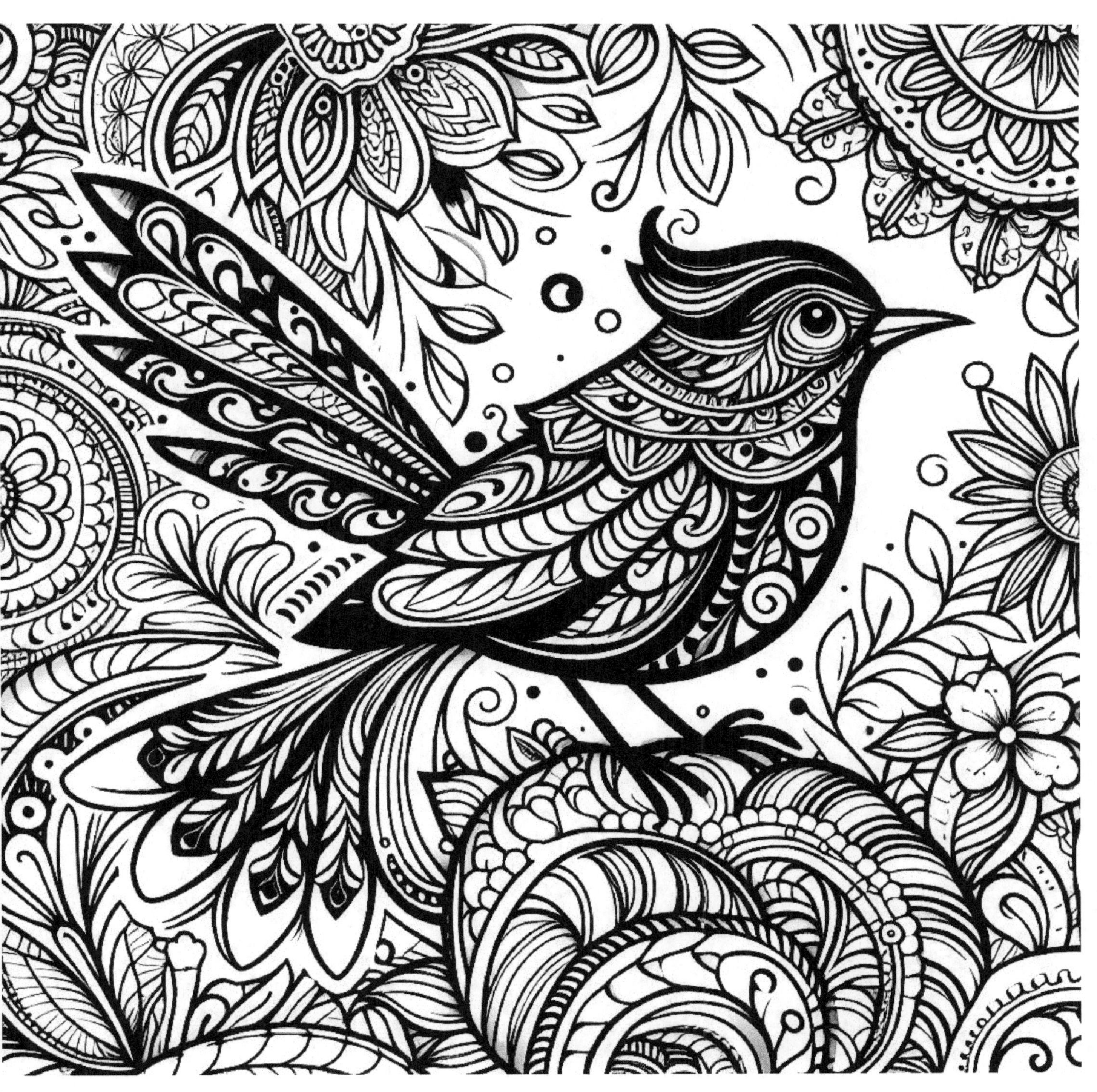

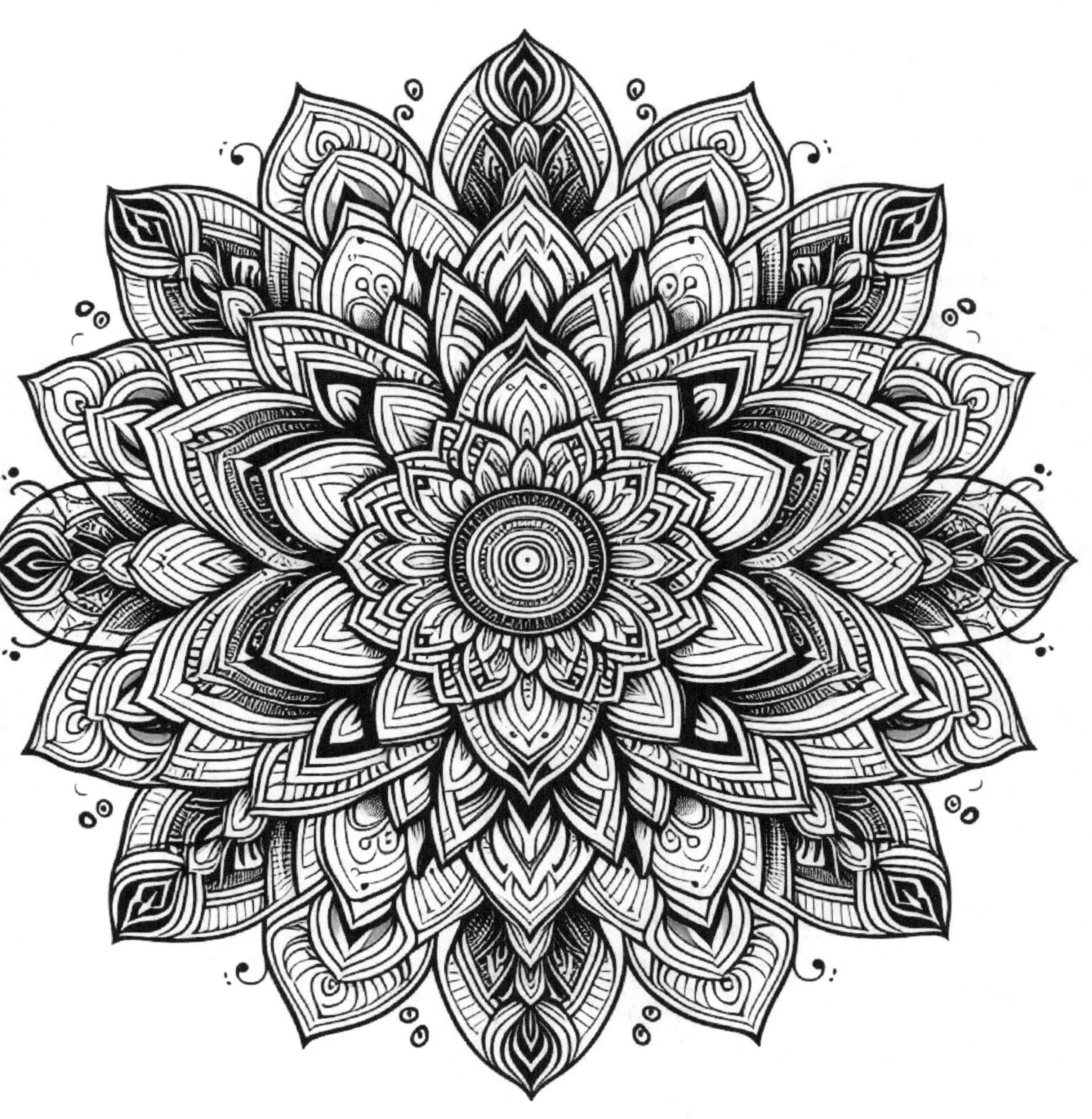

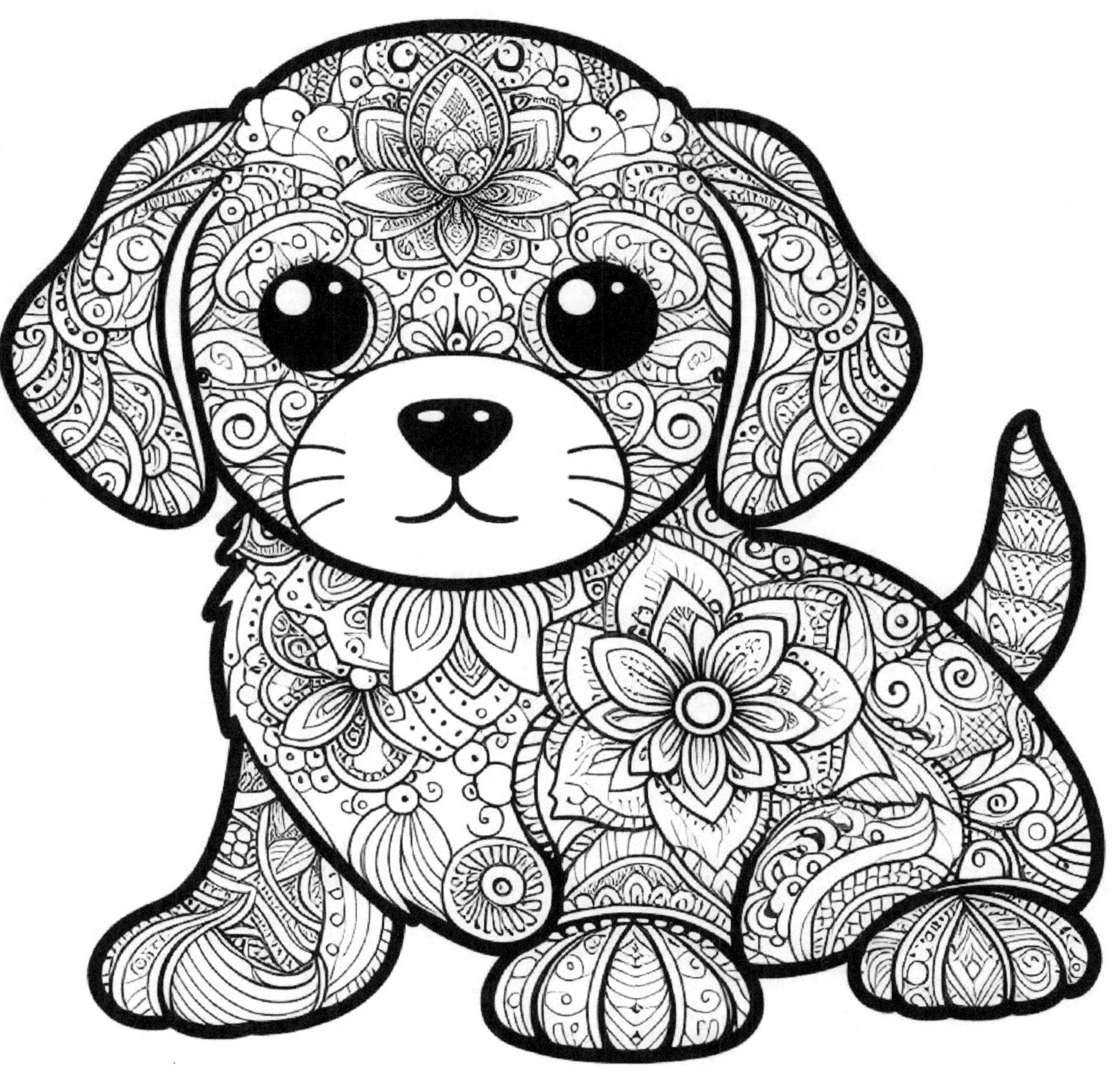

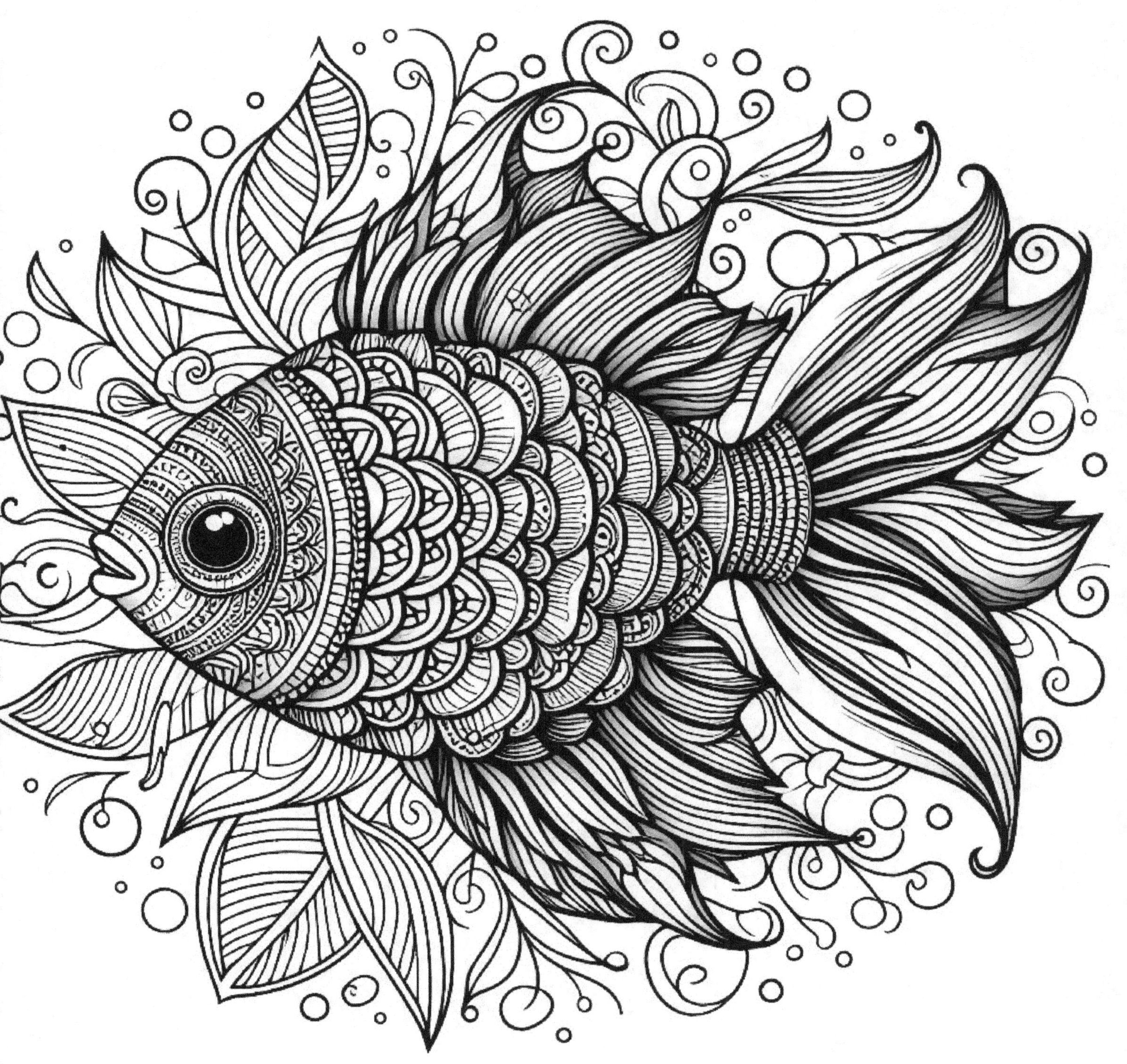

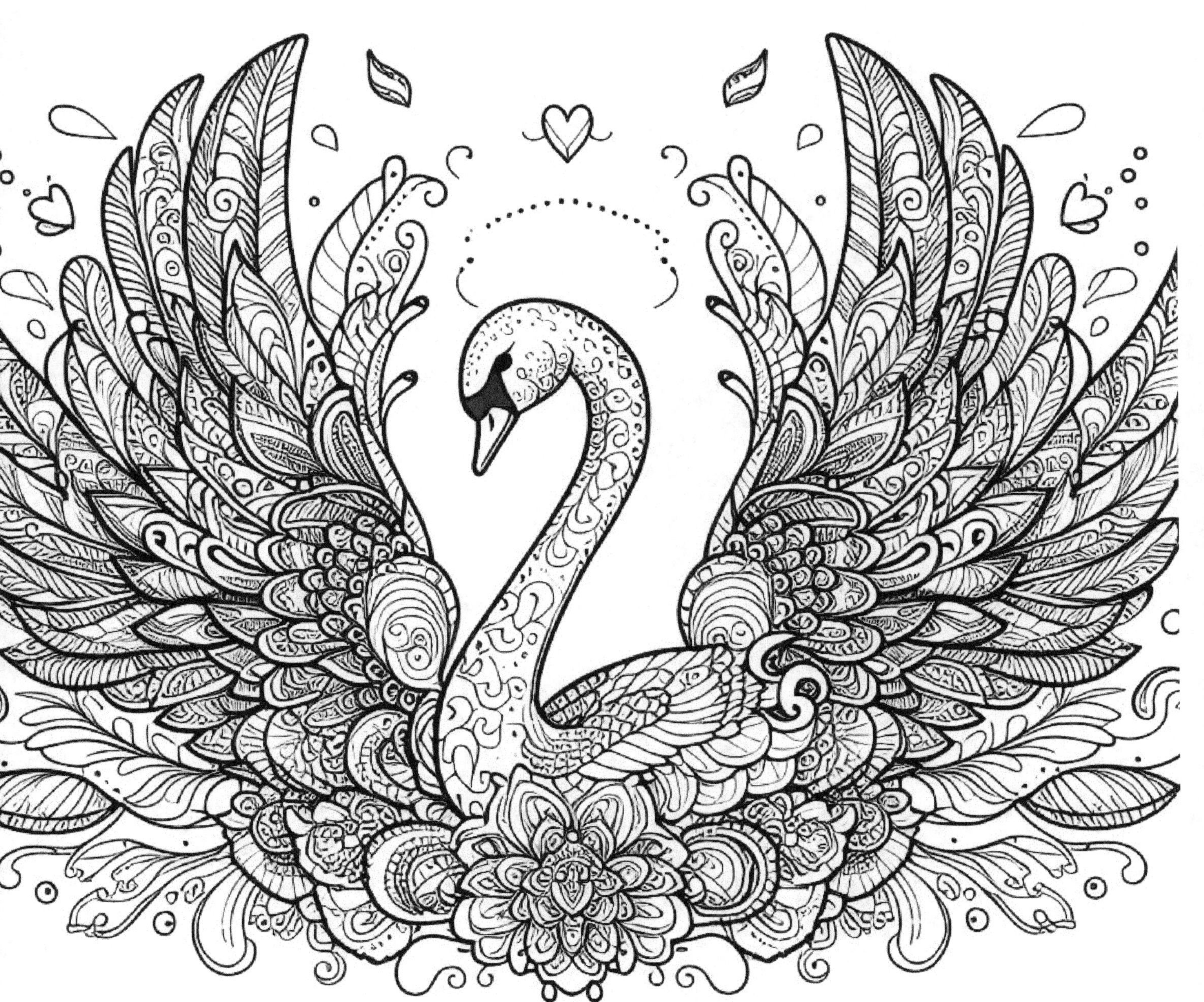

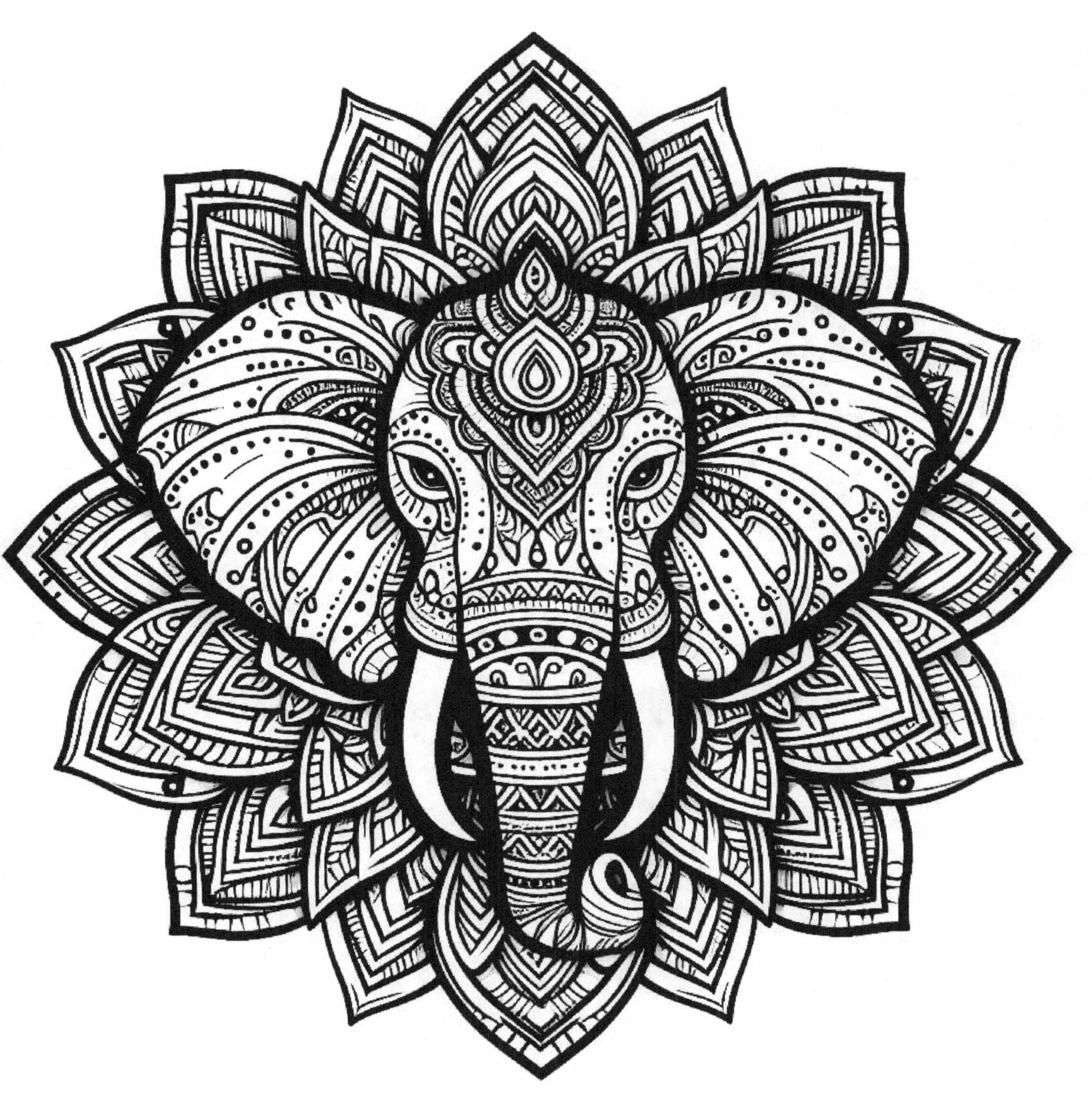

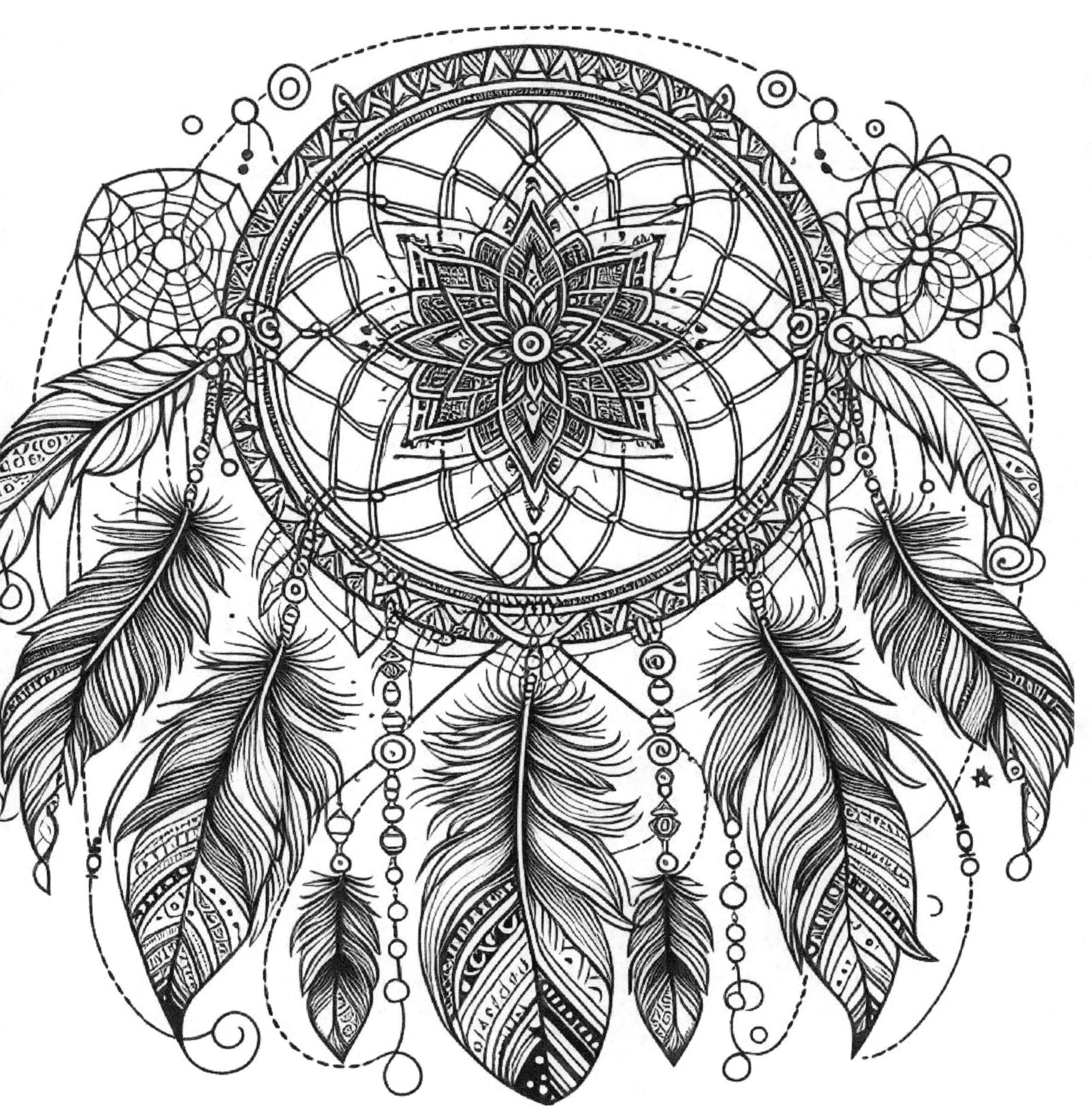

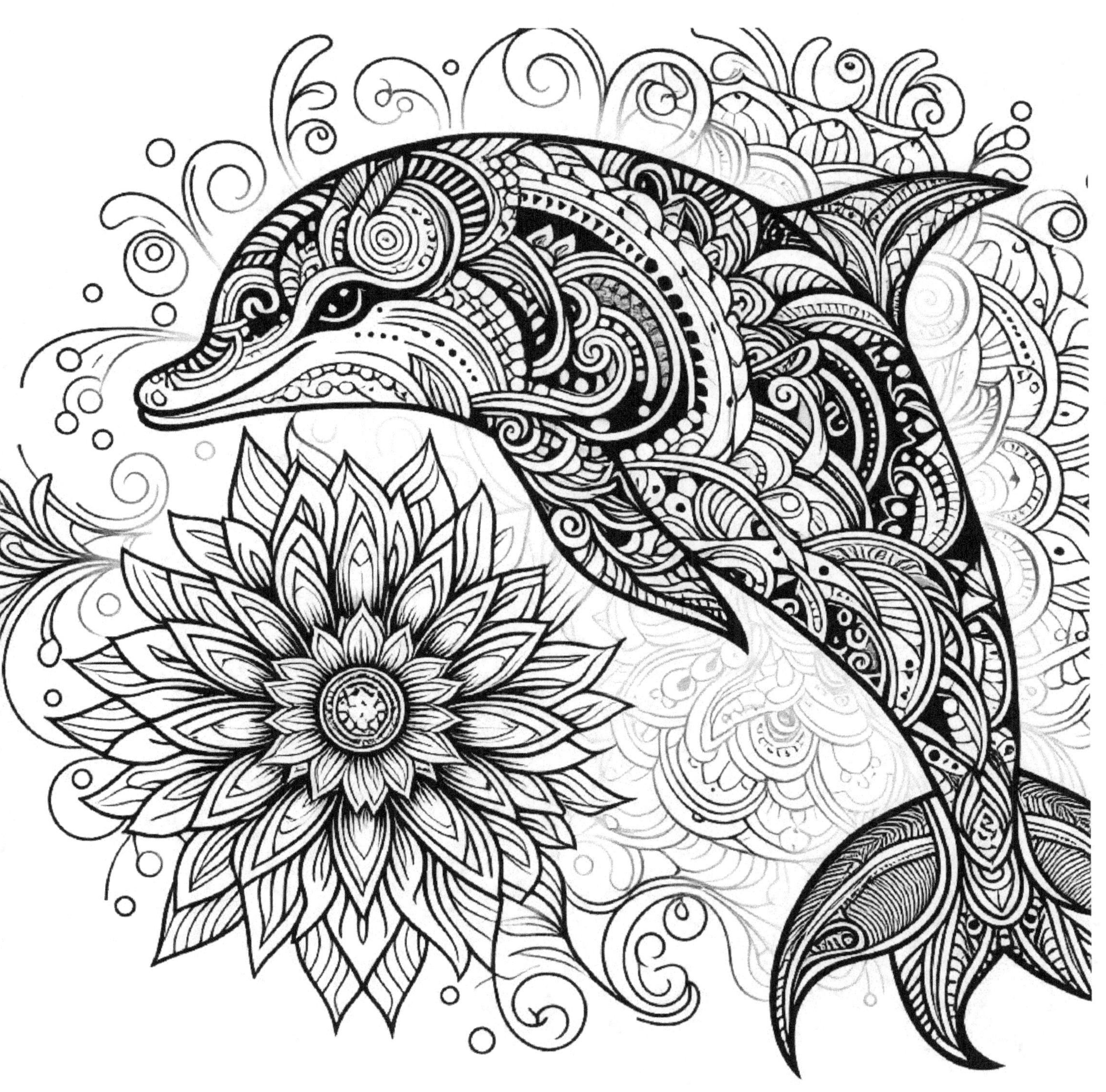

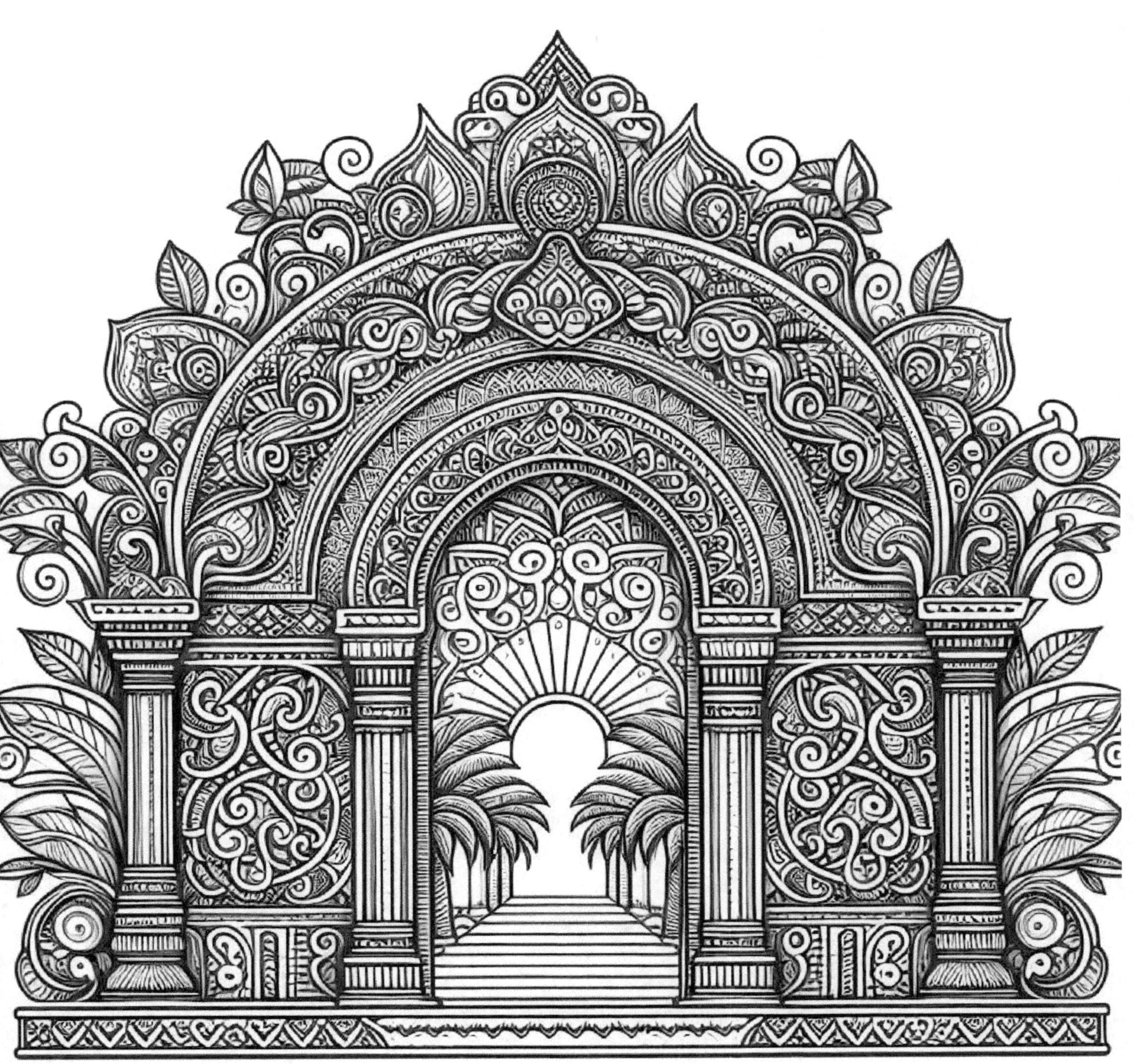

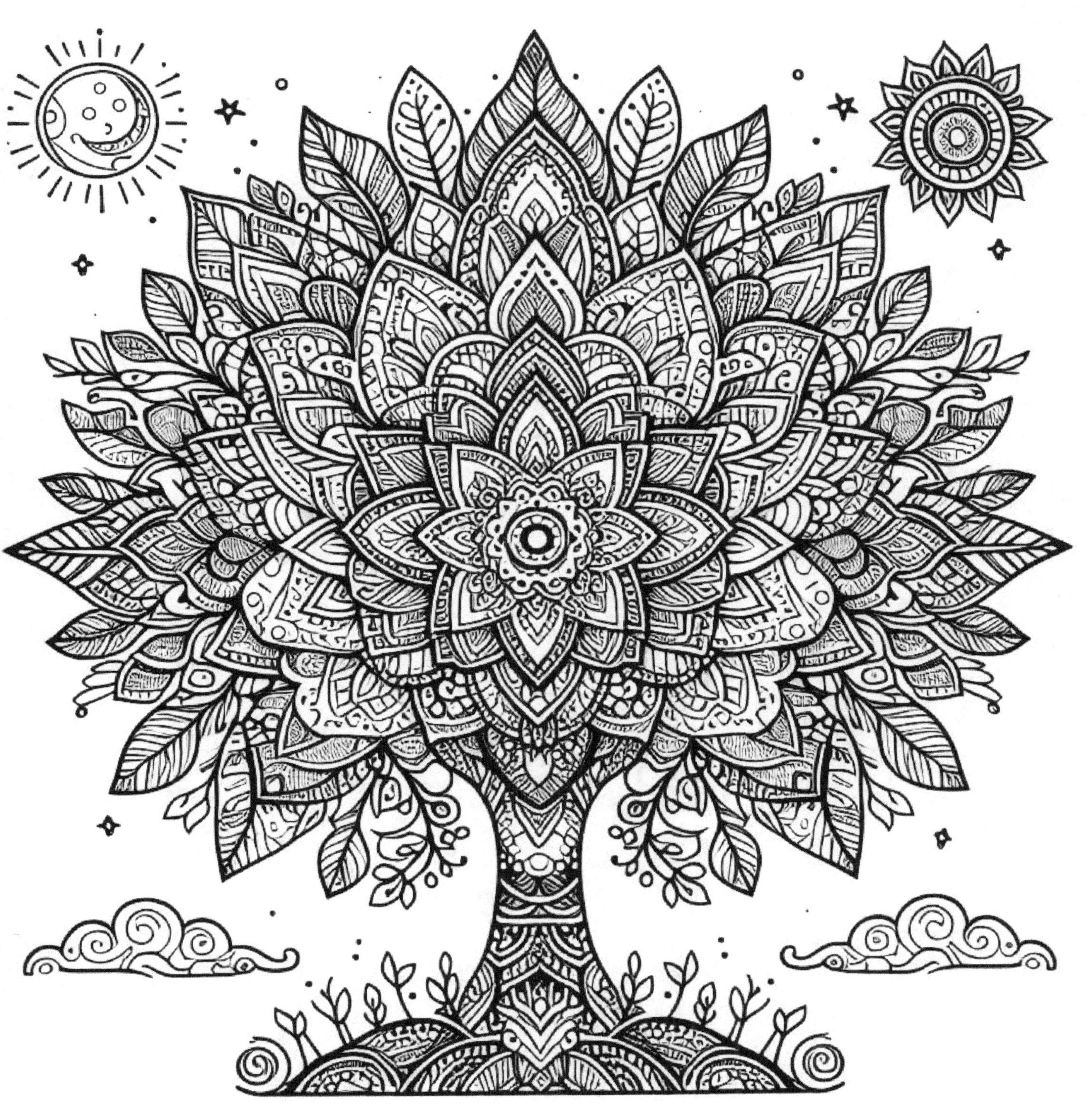

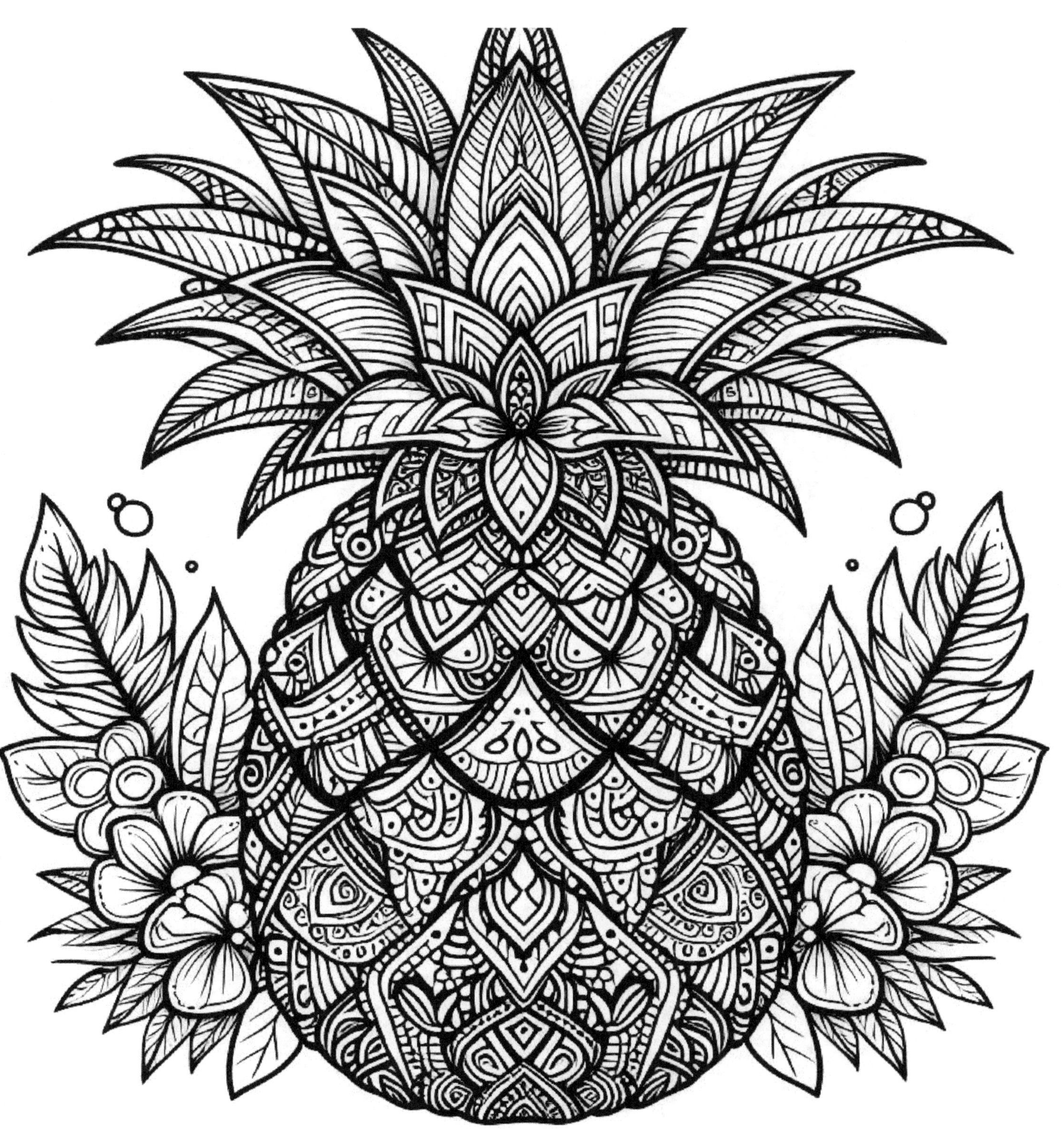

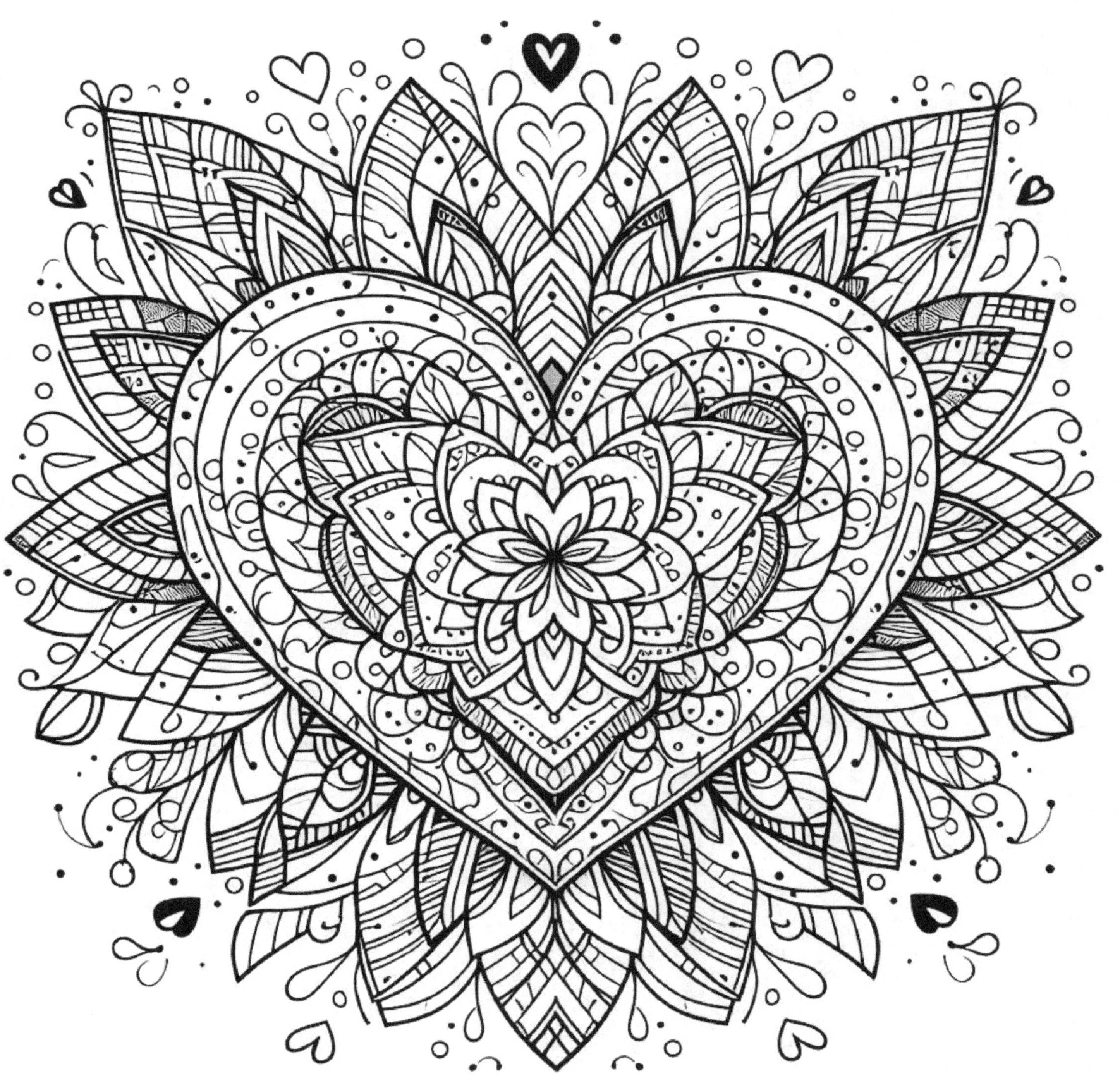

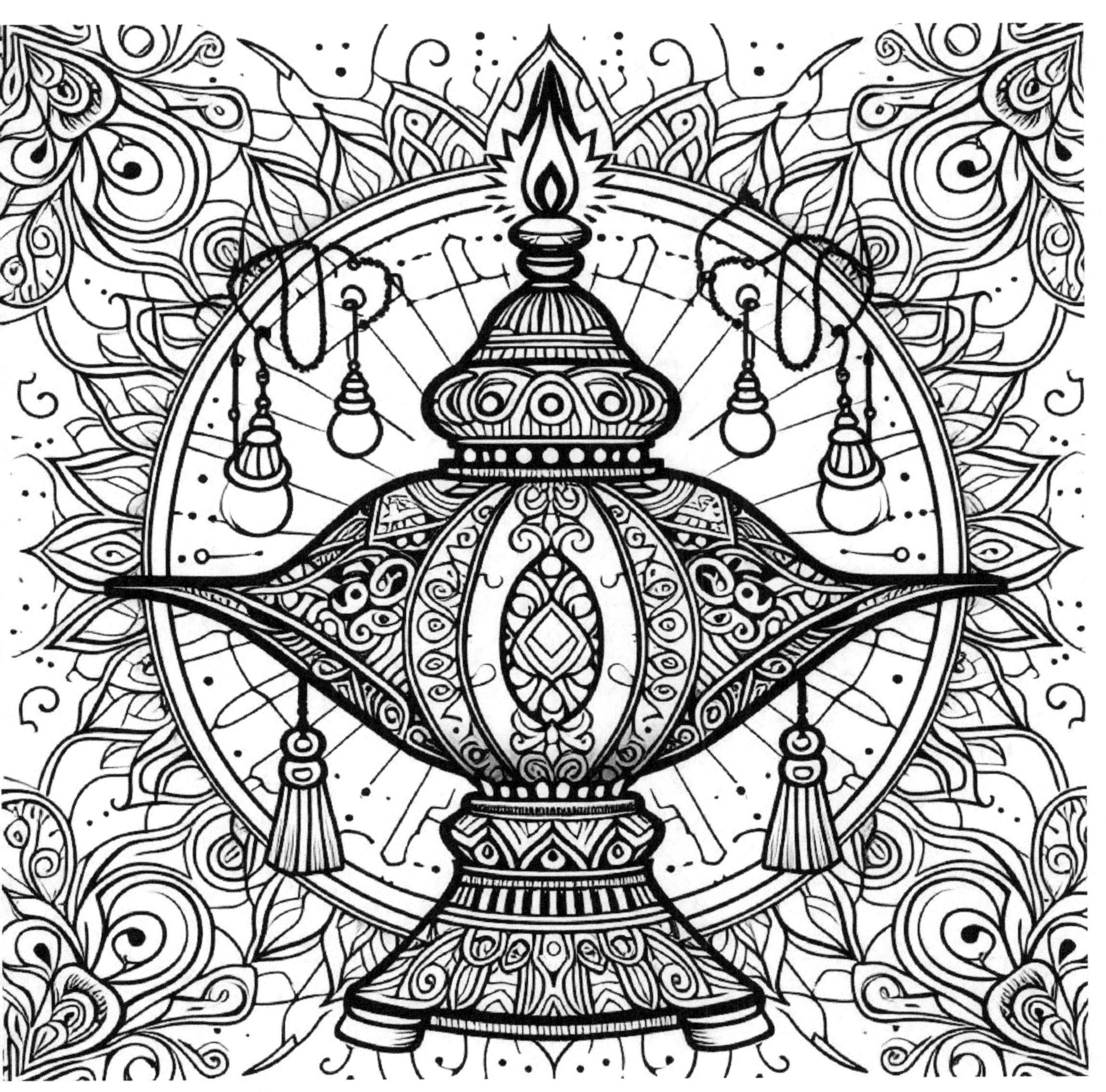

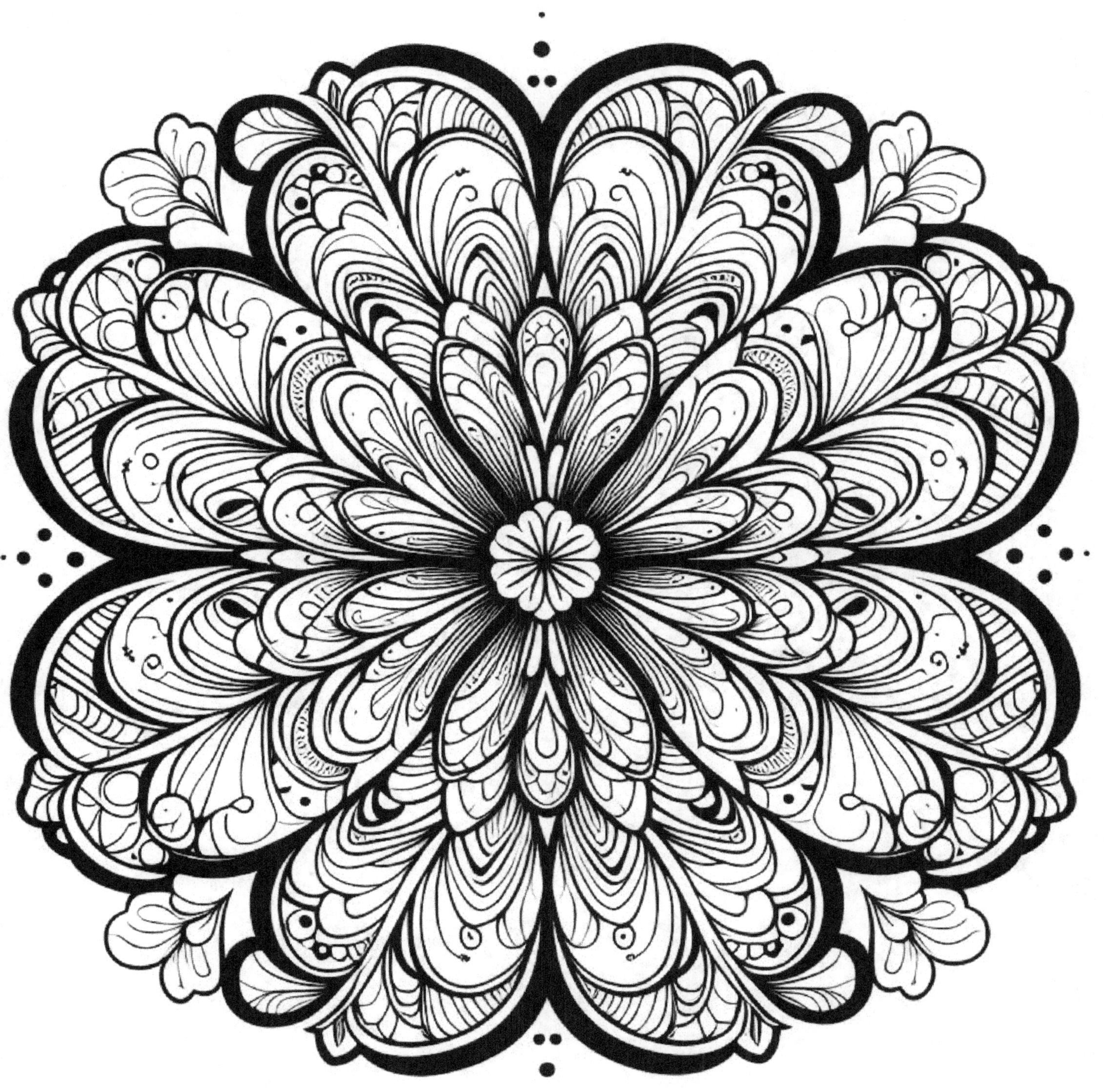

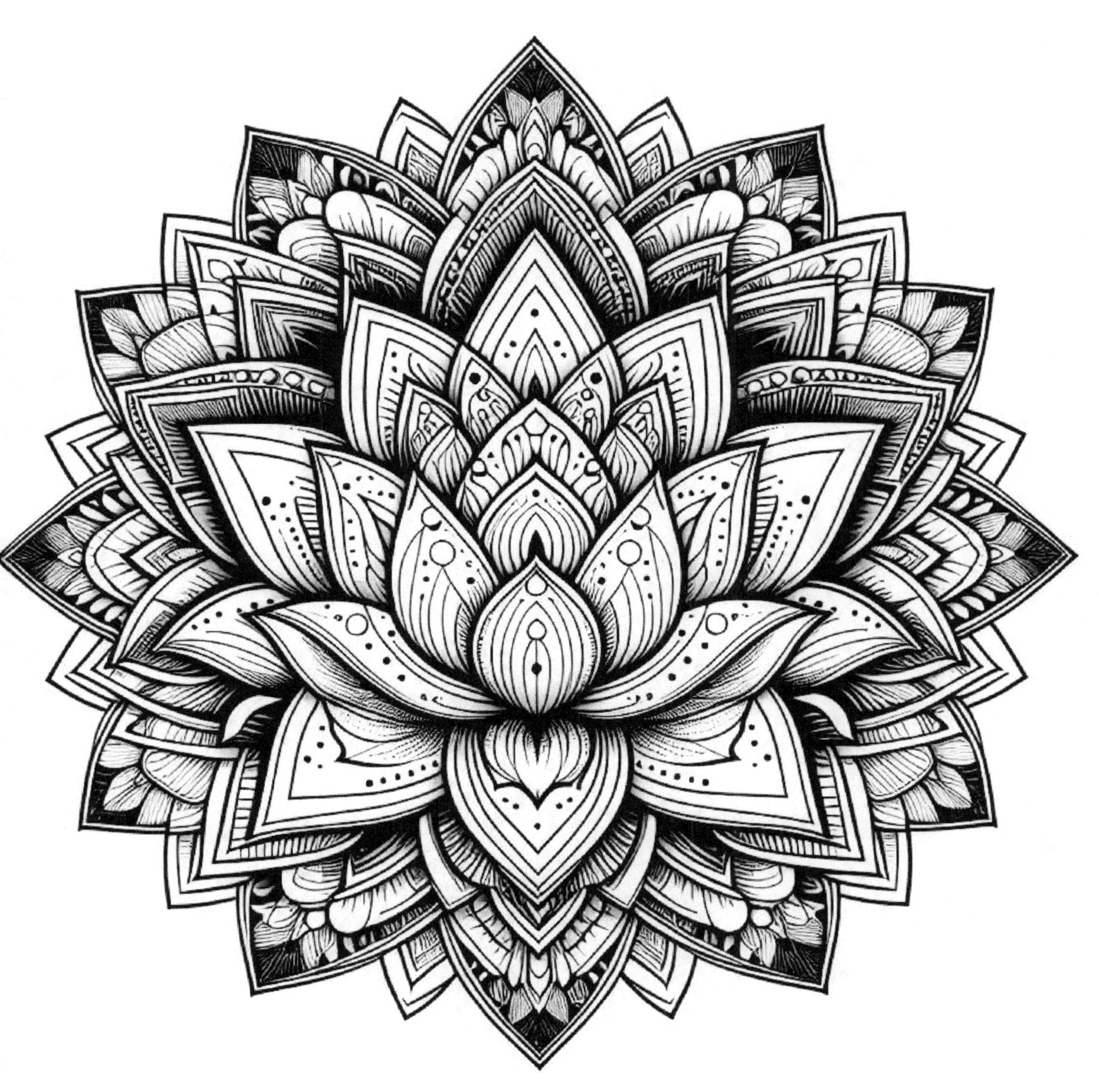

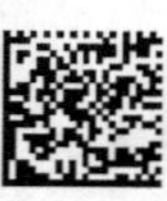

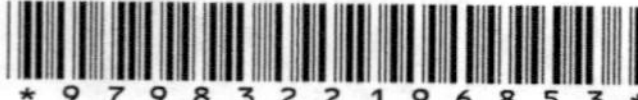
9 798322 196853